THE
SHELTER
OF
GOD'S PROMISES

PARTICIPANT'S GUIDE

SHEILA WALSH
WITH TRACEY D. LAWRENCE

THOMAS NELSON
Since 1798

NASHVILLE   DALLAS   MEXICO CITY   RIO DE JANEIRO

Published in Nashville, Tennessee, by Thomas Nelson. Thomas Nelson is a registered trademark of Thomas Nelson, Inc.

Quotes and excerpts have been taken from the trade book version of *The Shelter of God's Promises* © 2010 by Sheila Walsh. Used by permission. All rights reserved.

Thomas Nelson, Inc., titles may be purchased in bulk for educational, business, fund-raising, or sales promotional use. For information, please e-mail SpecialMarkets@ThomasNelson.com.

All Scripture quotations are taken from the Holy Bible, New International Version®, niv®. Copyright © 1973, 1978, 1984 by Biblica, Inc.™ Used by permission of Zondervan. All rights reserved worldwide. www.zondervan.com.

Other Scripture quotations are taken from the following sources: THE ENGLISH STANDARD VERSION (esv). © 2001 by Crossway Bibles, a division of Good News Publishers. HOLMAN CHRISTIAN STANDARD BIBLE (hcsb). © 1999, 2000, 2002, 2003 by Broadman and Holman Publishers. All rights reserved. NEW AMERICAN STANDARD BIBLE® (nasb). © The Lockman Foundation 1960, 1962, 1963, 1968, 1971, 1972, 1973, 1975, 1977, 1995. Used by permission. *The Message* (msg) by Eugene H. Peterson. © 1993, 1994, 1995, 1996, 2000. Used by permission of NavPress Publishing Group. All rights reserved. THE NEW KING JAMES VERSION (nkjv). © 1982 by Thomas Nelson, Inc. Used by permission. All rights reserved.

The Shelter of God's Promises Participant's Guide

ISBN: 978-1-4185-4606-9

Printed in the United States of America

11 12 13 14 RRD 5 4 3 2 1

THE PROMISE OF GOD'S SHELTER

Then the Lord said, "There is a place near me where you may stand on a rock. When my glory passes by, I will put you in a cleft in the rock and cover you with my hand until I have passed by."

—**Exodus 33:21–22**

CONTENTS

INTRODUCTION

I'm so glad you decided to make the commitment to take a deeper look at what Scripture has to say through this study, *The Shelter of God's Promises*. In the course of my work with Women of Faith, my daily walk, and living in community with other believers, I find that most of us are trying to make it through the storms of life with the wrong resources. As I have weathered my own storms, God has been faithful to bring me to a place where He has shown me the power of His promises. They are real. They are relevant. And they provide the foundation for daily confidence, joy, and hope.

I want to warmly welcome you, dear friend. I wish there was a way I could sit across the table from you and hear your own story. But I know that through this ten-week study, you will encounter many blessings that only God can give you. You will have the opportunity to hear stories of women in your groups, pore over the Scriptures together, and allow God to connect you to Him in ways that will strengthen you in this season of your life, whether you are in the middle of a storm or have come out on the other side.

I'm very excited about launching this study alongside my book *The Shelter of God's Promises*.[1] I encourage you to read the book with this study, but don't feel that you cannot participate if you haven't read it. The book and participant's guide work well together and reinforce all we will be discussing, but this study also stands independently.

There are ten promises we will look at in these weeks together:

1. The Promise of Jesus
2. The Promise of Provision
3. The Promise of Peace
4. The Promise of Confidence
5. The Promise of Love
6. The Promise of Grace
7. The Promise of Hope
8. The Promise of Strength
9. The Promise of More
10. The Promise of Home

In this study, we're going to look at what God has promised us, what those promises mean, and how our encounters with Christ are the eternal fulfillment of His unrelenting commitment to us. We're going to study some of the Bible's most compelling stories and look at how God's promises secure our lives even during the most difficult times.

OUR APPROACH

My heart is for women to dig deep into the Word of God. My hope for you is that you gain more knowledge about the Bible, but more than that, that you would discern what the Lord is speaking to you in a clearer way because you have spent time with Him. The Shepherd has a way of knowing the touch we need, no matter what day of the week it is. So my prayer is that His truth will move beyond head knowledge toward the heart, where faith is lived out. With that prayer committed to God, I want to introduce the sections to you.

STUDY FORMAT

Each week, there are five daily lessons, giving you room to go back on the weekend to review as you focus on your church fellowship and worship on Sunday.

I want you to dig deep and really spend time in the Word as you come to understand the significance of God's promises for you. Don't rush! Savor the warmth of God's presence as you invite Him to show you the blessing of His shelter.

There are two "tracks" for this study. Day 1 is the group study format, and days 2 through 5 are the personal study. There is a measure of consistency to each day's study, but we have allowed some variation throughout the week.

Group Study—Day 1

Your weekly group gathering will take around one and a half hours to complete, including the twenty-five-minute video.

Video

Each week, we will start with a video segment that will serve as the main focus for the study group. Summary points with fill-in-the-blanks and some key concepts are included for you to complete as you follow along with the video.

Small Group Discussion

Following the video, you'll see a section of small group discussion questions. Let these questions take you deep as you discuss God's promises with fellow believers. Learn from those who have been given different experiences with God's promises.

Looking Deeper

In this section you will learn the context of the week's promise in Scripture. You will examine key people, places, and background information.

Personal Reflection

At the end of day 1, you'll find a personal question to ponder as you launch into the week's study. Take time to consider what God has for you to learn this week, and then share your insights with your small group, if you feel comfortable doing so.

Living the Promise

Each week includes a practical application exercise for you and your group to accomplish during the week. Keep one another accountable as you continue to gather together.

Prayer

The group discussion time each week will conclude with a time of prayer. Through this study, I want to stress the importance of prayer as our lifeline to God's grace.

Personal Study—Days 2 through 5

The following exercises are found throughout the personal study lessons on days 2 through 5 for each promise. They may not each occur in each day's lesson, but you'll see them throughout each week's study.

Reconnecting with the Promise

Think of this as your warm-up exercise, to get the cogs turning and moving in the direction of the promise to be studied. We will be looking at many Bible verses over the course of this study, so we don't want to lose sight of the main promise for each week.

Understanding God's Promises

As the week goes on, you will study relevant passages of Scripture that are tied to the promise. You will examine key people, places, and background information. This is where we really engage our minds to give us a strong foundation on the week's concept. Then we'll begin to take steps to connect to the weekly promise in a more personal way. This is a place to engage the mind and heart together.

Embracing the Promise

This closing section will have takeaway value beyond this study, in that it may require self-examination or help you make a real-life choice you've been struggling with. This exercise will train us to be open to God's leading and to live prayerfully. This is where we can apply what we are learning and really see God's promises at work in us.

Prayer

There are prayer prompts at the end of each daily lesson as well as reminders along the way not to forsake a posture of prayer. Let God's Spirit speak to you so that you may listen, pray, pause, and be renewed during this time you've set aside in prayer.

I hope you find this study feeds you in the ways you need. You may want to prayerfully invite someone who is in need of encouragement to join you in this study. I know God will be faithful to shelter us in the midst of any storms ahead.

With conviction I say to you: "For no matter how many promises God has made, they are 'Yes' in Christ. And so through him the 'Amen' is spoken by us to the glory of God" (2 Corinthians 1:20).

May God richly bless you,
Sheila

THE PROMISE OF JESUS

I NEED SOMETHING TO HOLD ON TO

For no matter how many promises God has made,
they are "Yes" in Christ. And so through him the
"Amen" is spoken by us to the glory of God.

—2 Corinthians 1:20

JESUS IS THE PROMISE

For no matter how many promises God has made,
they are "Yes" in Christ. And so through him the
"Amen" is spoken by us to the glory of God.

—2 Corinthians 1:20

For many of us, the word *promise* is a reminder of how people are unfaithful or relationships disappoint. But I want to look at what the Bible says a promise really is: Jesus is the Promise in the flesh. Let this definition really sink deep into your mind and heart. Jesus is the Promise, and all His promises are true. When we believe God's promises, we are standing in agreement with Jesus that He is who He says He is and that He can be trusted with every part of our lives.

VIDEO
25 MINUTES

Watch session 1 on the Shelter of God's Promises *DVD. Keep your Bible nearby for reference and take notes in this book as needed. Fill in the blanks below as you listen to Sheila's message.*

- "For no matter how many promises God has made, they are '_____' in _____" (2 Corinthians 1:20).

- No matter what might be raging around you right at this very moment, God promises _____ and _____ when you're at your most _____ and _____.

- We can ____ a God who is _____ the entire universe together to _____ us together, even when everything seems to be falling apart.

- Our _____ does nothing to diminish God's _____.

- The Father is truly the only promise _____ who is _____ a promise _____.

KEY CONCEPTS

logos:

laminin:

MY NOTES

SMALL GROUP DISCUSSION
25 MINUTES

Break into small groups and discuss the following questions:

1. As you read the promise in 2 Corinthians 1:20, what hope and encouragement does this bring to your life right now?

2. What is there about this promise that challenges you?

3. Do you believe this promise is for you, for whatever you are facing right now?

4. Sheila told the story of a camping trip she took with her friends to the eastern Highlands of Scotland. She described the harsh realities of a storm she weathered. What are some of the harsh realities you've encountered in a recent "storm"?

5. What helped you navigate that storm?

6. What were some of the conditions of the storm or unexpected circumstances that threatened to keep you from relying on the promises of God?

> I made myself as comfortable as I could with my sleeping bag and settled in for the rest of the night. Although the wind kept howling outside, the cave was cut in such a way that I was completely sheltered. It was the unlikeliest of places, but when it seemed I was at my most vulnerable I found myself more secure than anywhere. That is how I embrace the promises of God. No matter what may be raging around you right at this very moment, God's promises offer shelter and cover when you feel most vulnerable and alone.
>
> —Sheila Walsh, *The Shelter of God's Promises* DVD

Bonus Question: What are some things God taught you after the storm was over?

LOOKING DEEPER

10 MINUTES

Dig deeper into Scripture to understand the context of this promise.

Now let's unpack 2 Corinthians 1:20, a verse that extends throughout this book: "For no matter how many promises God has made, they are 'Yes' in Christ. And so through him the 'Amen' is spoken by us to the glory of God."

The leaders of the church in Corinth were frustrated with Paul, and rumors were flying that Paul was fickle (2 Corinthians 1:17). They probably grumbled, "He promises to visit us and then changes his mind without even asking us!" Paul was hurt, and he defended himself in verse 17: "When I planned this, did I do it lightly?" Paul served God, and he knew it was critical that these believers knew that God is faithful. He wanted his actions to mirror Jesus', so that these brothers and sisters in Christ would know that God had been faithful to fulfill His promises in Jesus. You see, with God, there is no wavering between "yes," "no," and "maybe." There is nothing in His nature that is unreliable. And because God is faithful, we too can be faithful to follow Him.

But the fact remains that Paul was a man, and at times his plans might have changed by choice or circumstances beyond his control. That's why he was so insistent that the church understand that God is always and forever faithful. There is no uncertainty or confusion when it comes to Jesus' "yes" and "no." The Old Testament promises found their fulfillment in Him; Jesus is the personal guarantor of all the promises of God.

God is faithful, and He is covenant keeping. He is the only Promise Maker who is *always* a Promise Keeper.

PERSONAL REFLECTION

5 MINUTES

Meditate on the following question and hear what God is teaching you through His Word and through your study group. Share your insights with the group, if you feel comfortable doing so.

"Then they believed his promises and sang his praise" (Psalm 106:12). How would it impact your daily life if you were able to hold on to the promises of God each moment of each day?

LIVING THE PROMISE
5 MINUTES

Discuss ways to apply what you've learned this week with your group.

Think about the cultural voices that promise shelter in things other than God. For you, which "voice" is most tempting to listen to and competes with God's promises for your life?

PRAYER
5 MINUTES

Take time to pray with your group to close the session.

Focus on praying for God to open your hearts to receive His promises. Give thanks for Jesus' saving work on the cross.

> God's promise for you and me today is that there is a limit to the time that the enemy will be able to have free rein on this earth and that even during that limited time and space, Christ Himself will walk with us.
>
> —Sheila Walsh, *The Shelter of God's Promises*, chapter 1

DAY 2

SURVIVING THE BROKEN PROMISES

For no matter how many promises God has made,
they are "Yes" in Christ. And so through him the
"Amen" is spoken by us to the glory of God.

—2 Corinthians 1:20

❧ RECONNECTING WITH THE PROMISE ❧

When you hear the word *promise*, where does your mind wander? Do you think of a broken promise before you think of a promise kept? In the midst of struggle and disappointment, sometimes the promises we thought were a sure thing give way and we find ourselves alone. I know I've been there, and I'm sure you have too.

What is so painful about broken promises in our human relationships is that sometimes they make us question God's promises to us as well. So we have to allow God's promises to speak more loudly in us. One of the promises He deposited in my heart when I was baptized in my youth is a verse I still hold on to today:

> You did not choose me, but I chose you and appointed you to go and bear fruit—fruit that will last. Then the Father will give you whatever you ask in my name. (John 15:16)

🔲 What verse or verses do you hold on to when you are shaken to your core?

🔲 What pain do you carry as a result of a broken promise? Do you think you've allowed the pain to influence your heart more than God's promises? Explain.

⫸ UNDERSTANDING GOD'S PROMISES ⫷

There is a promise that runs throughout all the topics of this book, and it's found in Exodus 33:21–22. It's the promise of shelter, God's protection for our own good. Let's look a little more at the circumstances that led up to this promise. Read Exodus 32.

When Moses heard the promise from the Lord, he had spent forty days on Mount Sinai conversing with God. He heard the Law, and finally God handed him two stone tablets inscribed with the Ten Commandments by God's own hand. The experience was life changing. Then, at the end of that time, God instructed Moses to return to His people because they had fallen into sin.

Before leaving, Moses pled with God not to destroy them. "Then the LORD relented and did not bring on his people the disaster he had threatened" (Exodus 32:14). The Hebrew word for "relent" here is *naham*, which means "to change one's course of action." God was going to destroy those who rebelled against their covenant, His promise; but because of Moses' plea, He decided to have mercy.

Moses began his descent off the mountain, and he met Joshua, who had been standing watch over the people of Israel while Moses was away. They continued down the mountain, and as they approached the camp, they heard the people dancing and singing, worshipping an idol they had made.

Having just been in the presence of God's holiness, Moses responded to the Israelites' sin with passionate, righteous anger. He broke the stone tablets that were engraved with God's handwriting. Seeing that the people rebelled so fiercely against God's covenant, Moses burned their golden idol. Sadly, the Israelites broke their promise to God—specifically, the second commandment.

Later, in Exodus 33:18, Moses said, "Now show me your glory."

> Then the LORD said, "There is a place near me where you may stand on a rock. When my glory passes by, I will put you in a cleft in the rock and cover you with my hand until I have passed by." (Exodus 33:21–22)

This passage reveals God's great mercy. He not only spared the lives of His sinful people, but He extended great favor when He gave Moses this special privilege. Who wouldn't want to be shown God's glory? Moses alone witnessed this wondrous sight. How incredible!

KEY PLAYERS OF THE PROMISE

Moses—served as a prototype of Jesus and His plan for our salvation. He was the mediator of the covenant of the Law.

Aaron—a leader who did not display great strength of character; yet, because he was a witness to God's great love and mercy, he would prove to be the best-suited high priest. He knew, from this point on, how to deal gently with those who strayed away from God (see Hebrews 5:2).

Israelites—The Israelites' rebellion against God is no different from what believers experience today. We see ourselves in their story of surviving broken promises.

The Israelites had abandoned their faith and their leader, worshipping an idol that suited their own desires. They broke their promises when they let go of their faith in the one true God. But God's faithfulness never ended, and He responded to the sin of the people with blessing and protection.

Even though the Israelites had a history of breaking their covenant with God, God continued to show them mercy over and over again.

1. What does this passage reveal about God and how He relates to His people even when they are rebellious?

2. Reflect on a time when God showed you profound mercy even when you knew you didn't deserve it. How did this affect your response to God?

In this passage, Moses knows the LORD is angry at the Israelites. And Moses does the unthinkable—he tries to pacify the Lord:

> But Moses sought the favor of the LORD his God. "O LORD," he said, "why should your anger burn against your people, whom you brought out of Egypt with great power and a mighty hand? Why should the Egyptians say, 'It was with evil intent that he brought them out, to kill them in the mountains and to wipe them off the face of the earth'? Turn from your fierce anger; relent and do not bring disaster on your people. Remember your servants Abraham, Isaac and Israel, to whom you swore by your own self: 'I will make your descendants as numerous as the stars in the sky and I will give your descendants all this land I promised them, and it will be their inheritance forever.'" Then the LORD relented and did not bring on his people the disaster he had threatened. (Exodus 32:11–14)

God said to Moses, "What you ask I will do." If there was ever a time a prayer was not deserving of an answer, it was at this moment. Yet He did answer, and He revealed His glory to Moses. *Glory* refers to the complete power of God, His perfection, and the radiance of His person. Moses was allowed to experience this without being taken from this world.

However, God told Moses that He would protect him from the most powerful force man could ever face: the presence of God. The Lord stepped forward in Moses' behalf to protect him from Himself. There was no way Moses could stand before a completely holy God. Exercising abundant love and mercy, God hid Moses in the cleft of the rock and covered him with His hand, then His glory passed in front of Moses.

Ultimately, however, this promise was fulfilled through the work of Jesus on the cross. The promise God made to Moses to reveal His glory was finally manifested—made "Yes!"—in His Son. It's a privilege to be on this side of history, where we can see the crystal clear fulfillment of God's promises.

Moses showed a great deal of boldness with God. He knew what intimacy with God was like; therefore, he knew he could be completely honest in his requests. We can approach God in this same way. God shields us by bringing us closer to Him. He wraps Himself around the one He loves and holds him within the radius of His glory and power. Because He holds the one He loves close, nothing can penetrate that shield of protection, the shelter of God.

3. Moses shows us the story of redemption in many ways. He knew God's people well, and he was aware that they were in desperate need of a merciful God. In what ways are you in need of God's mercy today?

≫ EMBRACING THE PROMISE ≪

Approach God with boldness today. Ask Him to bless you by revealing His glory to you. Recognizing that God has shown you profound mercy, what can you do to share His mercy with others this week?

≫ PRAYER ≪

Lord, I often forget that Your promises surround me with Your mercy every day. Thank You that mercy is here for me today, that You know me by name and You protect me with Your hand. Show me today that I'm surrounded by Your mercy, and may Your voice be the loudest voice I hear. Fortify my heart with Your promises. In Jesus' name, amen.

DAY 3

THE THREAT OF A STORM

For no matter how many promises God has made,
they are "Yes" in Christ. And so through him the
"Amen" is spoken by us to the glory of God.

—2 Corinthians 1:20

⫷ RECONNECTING WITH THE PROMISE ⫸

In some key moments in my past, I wasn't well prepared to face certain storms because I didn't take time to read the clouds or know where the storm was coming from. Sometimes this information helps us to know how to respond more effectively, but other times there is no way to know until the storm has blown over. So as God's children, we need to know how to weather storms and endure the threatening waves that pass over us.

▦ Think about the last storm you came through or the one you are in now. Are you able to discern its source? Does that help or hinder your faith?

For me, choosing to study the promises of God in depth began with a letter. I get very few actual delivered-to-my-mailbox letters these days. Most of my friends communicate via e-mail or text message, so a handwritten envelope on my desk was something of a novelty. I picked it up and tore at its seams with curiosity. Then I began to read.

I have not met the woman who wrote to me, but apparently she once attended an event I had been speaking at and sensed a connection with me. She wrote about some of the struggles she had been through the few years prior. These were not small things: illness, financial hardship, and the breakup of her marriage. Amid her description of all these hardships, one line in the letter arrested my attention because of its profound simplicity: "I would not have made it this far without the promises of God."

🔲 Fill in the blank based on your experience: "I would not have made it this far without _____."

I thought of friends and others I've met in my thirty years of traveling the globe and speaking to groups around the world. I remembered people who have faced very similar, difficult circumstances and struggled to find hope in the middle of their mess. I read through notes left on my Facebook page, notes slipped into my hand at the end of speaking events. From the darkened caves of countless hearts I heard the same primal cry, the same questions over and over again:

> We can trust a God who is holding the entire universe together to hold us together, even when everything is falling apart. He is the Creator of you and me; and He is also the Sustainer of you and me.
>
> —Sheila Walsh,
> *The Shelter of God's Promises* DVD

Has God forgotten me?

Does my life matter?

Is there a plan somewhere in all of this mess?

How am I going to make it?

What will happen to me when I die?

What if I outlive my children?

How do I know that God even heard my prayer?

All of these questions reflect thoughts that are normal to have when the threat of a storm is looming. But rather than being filled with only these questions, we need to be filled with God's promises when we need them the most. They help us before, during, and after the storm.

⋙ UNDERSTANDING GOD'S PROMISES ⋘

Read 2 Corinthians 11:23–33.

After reading Paul's account of his hardships, it's amazing to think that he survived! How did he even endure such brutalities? Though an ordinary person, like you and me, the apostle Paul was a walking miracle. Read over the text and identify the types of afflictions and hardships Paul suffered.

1. Paul names such diverse trials as toil and sleeplessness, hunger, difficult relationships, and humiliation. Of the items in Paul's honest summary in 2 Corinthians 11:23–28, which ones do you relate to most?

2. Paul even says in this passage that his talk, the boasting in trials, is crazy talk. One version says, "I am talking like a madman" (ESV). But he says it is necessary to demonstrate God's work in him. In what ways is Paul an antihero, according to the way we typically think of heroes?

3. Paul ends the passage by blessing God and praising Him, though his hardships were deep and severe. Read James 1:2–4. Compare James's response with Paul's response to troubles and hardships. How can we profit from the storms according to this passage?

⁂ EMBRACING THE PROMISE ⁂

When the threat of storm comes, we should remember these survival tips:

1. Trust in the Promise, Jesus.
2. Keep your gaze on Him.
3. Praise Him for the profit that will come from enduring hardship.
4. Find reason to be grateful in the midst of loss and pain.

As you reflect on these applications, assess which one is most difficult for you. Take a moment to pray for strength and ask God to help you grow joy in your heart even while you are experiencing hardship. Pray for the Spirit to protect you from any bitterness toward God.

⫸ PRAYER ⫷

Lord, seal Your Word in my heart today. Give me confidence in You as I endure this hardship that I know does not compare to the hope that awaits me. Help me to consider it pure joy as I face trials of every kind. Help me to know You are walking with me in the storm and I am never alone. Amen.

DAY 4

DELAYED PROMISES

For no matter how many promises God has made,
they are "Yes" in Christ. And so through him the
"Amen" is spoken by us to the glory of God.

—2 Corinthians 1:20

⫸ RECONNECTING WITH THE PROMISE ⫷

Sometimes the storms we encounter seem to last a lifetime. The Bible is full of men and women who had delayed answers, which probably felt much like delayed promises. I like how Exodus 33:17 reminds us that we have found grace in His sight and He does indeed know our names.

Sometimes it feels like God has forgotten our names and the delayed answer means God has abandoned us. Most of us know what it feels like to be forgotten and the anxiety that can grow from a lack of hope. Proverbs 13:12 tells us, "Hope deferred makes the heart sick, but a longing fulfilled is a tree of life." When we feel we are in a desert, it seems the enemy loves to use such times to weaken our faith, to cause us to doubt the faithfulness of God. It's easy to fall prey to believing God is neglecting us. This can happen when months drone on with no answer. Then years. And we find ourselves echoing Job's sentiments: "I cry out to you, O God, but you do not answer" (Job 30:20).

You may relate to Cynthia's story:

We've been in a desert for the past six years. It feels like a lifetime, and then I think of the Israelites and their forty years of wandering—how did they do it? My husband has been underemployed or unemployed for so long. I try to be encouraging but sometimes I struggle with respecting him. It's nothing he has done, but I think it's just resenting the weight of supporting our family—something I don't want to carry. I don't want to be the provider for our family. The stress weighs me down. I feel sick and anxious at times. In my heart I know that God is our Provider and He has proven this time and time again. But then my head starts to add the numbers up, and I see that there is no way we can make ends meet each month. I don't want to go through this time and see nothing better in myself or my husband.

Cynthia's struggle may be similar to yours, or perhaps your wait extends for decades. I want to focus on examining our posture in the waiting period. No doubt, we will have moments when we question, *Can any good come out of this?* Part of coming through these hard questions is realizing our hope is misplaced or we don't believe God's plan is best for us.

🔲 What questions come to mind when you feel you're in a holding pattern of delayed answers from God?

⫸ UNDERSTANDING GOD'S PROMISES ⫷

Read Jeremiah 29:10–14.

Jeremiah was an extraordinary leader writing to the captives of Babylon. He admonished them to move ahead with their lives and to pray for those who enslaved them. Jeremiah taught the people that life cannot come to a grinding halt when we don't see immediate answers or solutions to our problems. Jeremiah's audience struggled to see hope at the end of their journey. The kingdom of Judah as they had known it could never be the same after the Israelites' seventy-year exile. They had suffered a tremendous amount of loss. They were weary.

Nebuchadnezzar, king of Babylon, had invaded Judah in 605 BC, and then in 597 BC took captive many important leaders, including Daniel and Ezekiel. Now under Nebuchadnezzar's reign, God was calling them to live peacefully under new rule. Their mandate was to survive and even flourish. Meanwhile, God said that He would be with them, their children, and their grandchildren, and He would hear their prayers in exile. God did not forget His people, even though they were captives in Babylon. He planned to give them a new beginning and a new purpose.

1. During a time of delayed answers from God, what or who enslaved you? If you are facing such a time today, name the person or thing that has been a source of the bondage you feel. If it is a person, make a point to pray for him or her, even though it is difficult.

2. The call to pray (Jeremiah 29:12) is part of the process, and God promises to listen. Write out a prayer for today and share something with God that you really want Him to hear.

3. Jeremiah 29:11 is one of those promises we hear often. Take time to read it in a few different translations and note your new discoveries about this promise.

4. Finish this thought: "My hope and future with God is _____."

❧ EMBRACING THE PROMISE ❧

If you have not memorized Jeremiah 29:11, take some time to let it set deeply in your heart. If you do have it memorized, try learning another version to give you a fresh understanding of what God is really promising. To know our future is set with God and that He is faithful to complete whatever He has begun in us keeps us close to Him.

❧ PRAYER ❧

God, I fear I limit You by expecting certain answers to my requests. The Israelites were afraid of the unknown, but You restored them in Your way and Your time. Reveal my heart to me, and show me whether I am closing myself off to doors You have opened to fulfill Your promise. Show me how to thrive when the promise is delayed.

DAY 5

OUT-OF-REACH PROMISES

For no matter how many promises God has made,
they are "Yes" in Christ. And so through him the
"Amen" is spoken by us to the glory of God.

—2 Corinthians 1:20

❧ RECONNECTING WITH THE PROMISE ❧

In this first session of our study, we have taken in more than just this week's promise; we have looked at other promises that reinforce it. There are more than three thousand promises in Scripture for our spiritual nourishment. We've learned: Jesus is the Promise; we can weather and survive the broken promises that we've encountered; the threat of storms does not have to rob us of intimacy with God; and, thankfully, delay is not denial. Today we are going to focus on the promises God has spoken to us that seem out of reach.

Maybe when you read Bible verses such as "Forget the former things; do not dwell on the past. See, I am doing a new thing! Now it springs up; do you not perceive it?" (Isaiah 43:18–19), you think this promise is impossible—you can never be restored or healed from your past. Or maybe when you read Jesus' words, "I have overcome the world" (John 16:33), from your perspective the world has trampled on you and there is no sign of relief. The truth is, those impossible things in our lives are not impossible for God. Sometimes it will take a miracle, along with patience and perseverance. And sometimes the answer is a solution we never thought about. When God's answer comes, His creativity leaves us stunned and in awe of Him. We know it's Him because there is no other explanation for such a glorious solution. He loves to bring us toward His promises that seem out of reach because it always means there is room for Him to show up—we can't do it without Him. We are in a posture of humility in these times and we are desperately crying out to Him.

Yesterday we focused on the hope and future that God promises all of His children. Our futures are secure. But during a crisis, it is easy to make our temporal turmoil and pain bigger than God Himself, who is eternal. Sometimes the promises we long for seem out of reach, impossible even for God.

⫸ UNDERSTANDING GOD'S PROMISES ⫷

Read Luke 1:26–37.

The birth of Christ, the moment when God's promises took on human flesh, is full of challenges, leaps of faith, crisis, drama, and the impossible. Mary was faced with impossible circumstances and overwhelming conditions. Have you ever been there? A young Jewess, Mary was literally part of God's answer to the clutches of sin and death in this world, and she would have to endure judgment, resistance, and profound heartache in order to carry out God's plan.

It's interesting to note that no other book in the Bible is more dependent on the eyewitness accounts of women than the gospel of Luke. As a historian, Luke knew who to talk with to gather firsthand information. The author recognized the key role women played in the events of salvation throughout the book: the birth of Jesus, the crucifixion, and the burial and resurrection of Jesus. He built the picture that, during Jesus' earthly ministry, women were faithful followers and participants in serving Him. Sometimes as women, we forget that all God's promises are for us, too, as we try to discover our particular calling and role in our churches, communities, and families.

The text says Mary was "highly favored" by God (Luke 1:28). In order to believe this would all come to pass, that the Savior of the world would be born through her womb, Mary had to cling to the words promised to her. That was what kept her heart alive with faith to believe. The angel's pronouncement prompts the question in Mary, "How will this be, since I am a virgin?" (v. 34). The conception occurs when the Spirit overshadows her, and she is given a sign, a promise of support—her relative Elizabeth.

If ever there was a promise that was too far-fetched to believe, it was the promise of Mary conceiving the Savior of the world. Jesus is the Promise, and Mary was the first to believe that Jesus was the fulfillment of the Promise, that God always does what He says He will do (2 Corinthians 1:20). As Mary cradled the "Yes" of God in her arms, her spirit whispered, "Amen."

1. What promise of God seems out of reach to you today? Write out what needs to happen for this promise to be fulfilled. What verse or verses speak to this promise?

2. Often when a promise *is* or *seems* impossible, God gives us support. Read about Mary's visit to Elizabeth (Luke 1:39–56). How did God offer tremendous support through this relationship? What were the impossible elements in Elizabeth's own story?

3. Mary answered the angel by saying, "May it be to me as you have said" (v. 38). Are you able to say this with conviction in your own situation? Why or why not? What makes it difficult to resign yourself to God's complete will for you, to give full submission to Him?

4. Think about those in your path. Who has God providentially placed in your life to support you while you try to reach for the impossible?

⫸ EMBRACING THE PROMISE ⫷

You may be in a place where you are praying to God for a miracle. Praise God you are praying to the only God who can perform miracles! God created the earth when the atmosphere was "formless and empty" (Genesis 1:2). God alone is able to create something out of nothing! In this season of life, the biggest mountain may be in front of you and you have no idea where to turn. In this session's video and in the introduction to *The Shelter of God's Promises*, I made reference to Psalm 121: "I lift up my eyes to the hills—where does my help come from? My help comes from the LORD, the Maker of heaven and earth" (vv. 1–2). I love how the Holman Christian Standard Bible translates verse 5: "The LORD protects you; the LORD is a shelter right by your side."

This psalm is written from a weary traveler's perspective. All of us are on a journey in which we will encounter storms, treacherous terrain, and steep mountains. Pilgrims must travel through lonely country to their destination, where they are protected, not by anything earthly, but by the Creator Himself. Christ not only comes to fulfill the promises of God, but He is our ever-present shelter in the storms of life.

Let the promise of His help restore you today. His arm is long enough to reach around the mountain and hold you (or move you or the mountain, whatever is required to fulfill His plan for your life).

⫸ PRAYER ⫷

Lord, You are faithful to me, and I praise You for the promises You are fulfilling through me. Your Word has touched me and changed me this week. Keep growing my heart with Your promises. Seal this promise in my heart. There is a place near You where I can stand, whether I face broken promises, struggle with delayed promises, or am trying to reach for something that seems impossible. I stand with You and know my future is secure.

THE PROMISE OF PROVISION

I DON'T HAVE ENOUGH

And my God will meet all your needs according
to his glorious riches in Christ Jesus.

—**Philippians 4:19**

DAY 1

THE PROMISE OF PROVISION

And my God will meet all your needs according
to his glorious riches in Christ Jesus.

—**Philippians 4:19**

Are you feeling antsy and unsure, stressed about your day, your week, your month? Perhaps you rolled out of bed this morning and your thoughts quickly went to how you might come up short for the day—what you don't have. Sometimes we are overcome by what we lack and before we can even clear our heads of the fog of sleep, we are trying to come up with ways to find the thing we *need*.

The truth is that God knows our every need and has been proven to provide abundantly beyond what we can rightly expect. How do we know that? Think of the abundant grace of Christ's gift of His own life for us. How can we not trust in such a provision and such a Provider?

VIDEO

25 MINUTES

Watch session 2 on the Shelter of God's Promises *DVD. Keep your Bible nearby for reference and take notes in this book as needed. Fill in the blanks below as you listen to Sheila's message.*

- "And my God will meet all your _____ according to the riches of His glory in _____ _____." (Philippians 4:19)

- It's important to note that Paul refers to their _____, but he makes no mention of their _____. There is a chasm of difference between what we need and what our culture has lulled us into wanting.

- God knows our every need and has been proven to _____ abundantly beyond what we can rightly _____.

- _____ is when we partner with God to bring about His _____ for our lives.

- "I am the bread of life" means "I am your _____ for _____."

KEY CONCEPTS

riches (in the context of Philippians 4:19):

glory (in the context of Philippians 4:19):

Jehovah Jireh:

Bethlehem:

> God is faithful, and His provision will be in keeping with the wealth of His mercy demonstrated in Jesus Christ.
>
> —Sheila Walsh, *The Shelter of God's Promises* DVD

MY NOTES

SMALL GROUP DISCUSSION
25 MINUTES

Break into small groups and discuss the following questions:
In the video segment, Sheila raises this question:

Have you ever noticed that when God supplies what we need, there is deep gratitude and contentment, but when we reach out simply for what we want, it never quite fulfills us? We're always left feeling as if we want more.

1. Describe a time when you received something you thought you needed, but it didn't fulfill you and you still felt the ache of desire.

2. Discuss why things that are simply desires aren't necessarily bad. How can we discern between desires that are valid and desires that are self-centered?

3. In one word, describe a need you have today. Expound as you feel appropriate.

Haven't you been there, that place of worry, fret, and fear when the provisions needed aren't at hand and aren't coming? Or maybe you've been in that place where there is a circus going on around you, with all kinds of things coming your way, just not what you really needed. You get lost in a pile of bills, feeling overwhelmed with everything that has to be taken care of and not enough resources to meet the needs. The demands of life can be overwhelming when you look at what you have and compare it to what you need. You can be left to wonder: *Is God listening? Does He see? Will He fix things?*

—Sheila Walsh, *The Shelter of God's Promises*, chapter 2

4. Look honestly at yourself and answer this question: Do you trust God to provide for your needs? Why or why not?

Bonus Question: Often, when our need is greatest, we neglect to go to our Father. Share some of the reasons that you don't go to Him, even though He is your Source.

LOOKING DEEPER
10 MINUTES

Dig deeper into Scripture to understand the context of this promise.
Read John 6:30–35.

> I am the bread of life. He who comes to me will never go hungry. (John 6:35)

Bread is an image we see throughout the Bible. It shows us God's merciful gift of sustenance, and we remember how much we need him when we're hungry for it. In the Old Testament, manna (what Jesus called "bread from heaven" in John 6:32) kept the Israelites alive in the wilderness. Likewise, it was prophesied that Jesus would be born in the town of Bethlehem, which means "house of bread." Jesus used a loaf of bread to feed and satisfy five thousand people, showing His divine power to the multitude. And finally, Jesus asked His disciples to remember His body broken as a loaf of bread would be, serving as the atonement for our sin.

He fulfills the desires of those who fear him; he hears their cry and saves them.
—Psalm 145:19

Jesus reminds us that His provision is something we need daily. We don't have to pray the perfect words, because He knows what we need before we even utter it. But He asks us to come to him because He knows that prayer brings us into right positioning with God. We are coming as His children, and He is our Source. He will always, always provide what we need.

PERSONAL REFLECTION
5 MINUTES

Meditate on the following questions and hear what God is teaching you through His Word and through your study group. Share your insights with the group, if you feel comfortable doing so.

Prayerfully think about this week's promise. Read Philippians 4:19, giving emphasis to different words (i.e., And *my* God will meet, And my God *will* meet . . .). Do this until you've reached the end of the verse.

How is the Spirit speaking to you individually about this promise? Which word emphasized is most alive in your heart today?

LIVING THE PROMISE
5 MINUTES

Discuss ways to apply what you've learned this week with your group.

Have you ever wanted something a friend had and thought God was being cruel to not supply it to you as well? Consider the ways this can affect your relationship with God and others, and write down three strategies you can take to stop negative thought patterns.

PRAYER
5 MINUTES

Take time to pray with your group to close the session.

Spend some time in prayer, expressing thanks for Jesus' undeniable provision in your life, most importantly the provision of salvation.

> Prayer is when we partner with God to bring about His will for our lives and when we are honest and say, *I cannot do this alone, and what I have isn't enough. Please provide.*
>
> —Sheila Walsh, *The Shelter of God's Promises* DVD

DAY 2

OUR NEEDS

And my God will meet all your needs according
to the riches of his glory in Christ Jesus.

—Philippians 4:19

≫ RECONNECTING WITH THE PROMISE ≪

Sometimes it's difficult to know our own hearts at times. Part of understanding the promise of God's shelter and understanding our needs begins with reflecting on the question, How did God create me, and what do I need in order to serve Him?

It's easy to think that all our desires will be satisfied if we had that "one thing" we lack. We think, *If I just had financial security, then I'd be set for life. Or I'd have the support I need if I could just find that friend who really understood me. Or If that one person would leave my department, I could be successful and then the boss would give me the promotion I need.* Our thought life reveals a lot about what we believe to be our needs.

God made us with physical, spiritual, and emotional needs. And the more we study Scripture, the more we see He is concerned with all of our needs. He fed the hungry, healed the sick, and freed those in spiritual bondage. God also knows exactly what *your* need is today. He specifically knows the touch you need from Him.

✍ In the chart below, name a need you have in each of the sections. For example, if you are struggling with hardship in marriage, you may feel some of your relational needs are unmet (emotional). Or you may have just lost your job and are struggling to figure out where money for groceries will come from this week (physical). No matter what you identify, we will focus in this chapter on the wonderful truth that God is our source for all of these real needs.

Spiritual	Emotional	Physical

⋙ UNDERSTANDING GOD'S PROMISES ⋘

Read Philippians 4:19.

KEY PLAYERS OF THE PROMISE

Paul—the great apostle who penned thirteen books in the New Testament; known as the disciple who would impact the fledgling church more than any man in history.

Philippian Christians—Paul knew God was his source for all he needed, and he shared his needs with this group of believers. They participated in being an answer to God's promise to provide for Paul. They supported Paul in carrying out the work of a missionary. Community often plays a role in our needs being met. Though God is our source for all things, He uses key people and resources to show His faithfulness toward us.

Paul wrote the book of Philippians to one of his favorite churches while under house arrest in Rome. The church had sent a dear brother, Epaphroditus, to encourage Paul in his prison. He wrote to thank them for their kindness and monetary support in this time of need. His spirits were lifted and he offered a sincere prayer from a love-filled heart for their blessing.

We find the image of "a fragrant offering" (Philippians 4:18) throughout the Old Testament, referring to a sacrifice that pleases God (Genesis 8:21; Leviticus 1:9, 13–17). Paul's joy is not simply that they cared for him; he's delighted that their giving enhanced their relationship with God, their Provider.

In this letter and other epistles, Paul used the term *koinonia* to express how grateful he was that his own needs, which were both financial and relational, were satisfied. The word *koinonia* is often rendered as "fellowship" or "partnership." It is used to explain the unique connection we have with Christ and other believers. Paul indicated in this letter that these particular believers had cared for and worked with him, helping meet his needs from the start as he spread the gospel. It's tempting to take this verse out of context and simply view it as an invitation to provide God with a list of everything we perceive we need. But after closer study of this passage, we'll see that Paul was sharing the secret to a contented life. In the act of giving, they had become more like Christ. They supplied his needs out of the little they had, knowing that God would supply their needs out of His glorious riches in Christ.

1. What does the Corinthians' giving tell us about their understanding of God as their Provider?

2. What would it look like for you to live the contented life that Paul describes in Philippians 4:11–13?

3. How does Paul's ability to receive their financial support speak to his humility?

Now let's look at another display of generosity from Paul's supporters, the Macedonian Christians, who were not a wealthy group.

Read 2 Corinthians 8:1–10.

Often God meets our needs when we are open to giving to others. We shouldn't wait to help someone else only when we have surplus. Roman custom encouraged the rich to act as patrons; they, in turn, would receive preferential treatment from their clients. Paul refused to play into this custom and was supported by his congregations and also through manual labor, so he wouldn't fall into partial relationships with wealthy donors.

4. Though you may be in a place where financial resources are tight, what are some ways you can help be an answer to the needs around you?

5. Paul writes in 2 Corinthians 8:9, "For you know the grace of our Lord Jesus Christ, that though he was rich, yet for your sakes he became poor, so that you through his poverty might become rich." What did Christ give up for us to meet our needs? (Also see Philippians 2 for further reflection.)

6. What are some needs Jesus has met for you throughout your relationship with Him? In what ways can you claim to be rich beyond monetary measurement?

7. Sometimes we have to swallow our pride in order to receive something God wants us to have. When has it been hard to receive from someone who wanted to meet your need?

⁂ EMBRACING THE PROMISE ⁂

Make a list of the things you desire in your life. Take a moment to pray for discernment about which items are *needs* and which are *wants*. Prioritize the needs, and ask God for provision. If you find you have no pressing needs, ask God to reveal the needs of others to you and look for ways to help those who are less fortunate than you.

⁂ PRAYER ⁂

Lord, You became poor so You could meet our every need. You left the right hand of God to save me. Thank You, God, for this promise, that You will supply all my needs according to Your glorious riches. I praise You that You know what my needs are better than I know them. Help me to know what I need and not just what I want.

Continue to pray and listen for the Spirit to speak to you.

DAY 3

PRAYING FOR DAILY BREAD

And my God will meet all your needs according
to his glorious riches in Christ Jesus.

—**Philippians 4:19**

⁂ RECONNECTING WITH THE PROMISE ⁂

Today we will look at the way Jesus instructed us to pray, "Give us today our daily bread" (Matthew 6:11), and how it relates to this week's promise. A big part of prayer is simply asking God for help. We know God knows our needs

> Prayer is daily admission of our need for God.

before we ask, but He still wants us to come to Him with everything. Sometimes we don't even ask our small groups or close friends for prayer because we wrongly assume they have enough trouble of their own. We don't want to bother others with our struggles. This attitude often flows over into our relationship with God.

What's the hardest thing for you about prayer? Is it discipline? Is it having faith that God hears you?

It sounds so easy, after all, when someone says, "Just believe in God's promises."

That kind of response is like the message in one of my favorite movies from when I was growing up, that black-and-white classic *I Remember Mama*, about a family of Norwegian immigrants living in San Francisco. The family was extremely poor and every purchase required a group decision. Whether deciding to buy a coat for one of the children or medicine for the cat named "Uncle Elizabeth," Papa brought out the money box and counted what was in there to see if it would be enough. Each time, the family discovered there was just enough and Mama said, "Good. We shall not have to go to the bank today." Surprisingly, as the movie comes to its climax (spoiler alert!), it's revealed that Mama and Papa did not have a single penny in the bank. They lived from day to day, moment by moment, sheltering their children from the truth.

It's wonderful to live out that kind of faith. The resolve of Mama and Papa in that movie has reminded me so much of my own childhood, where there was very little to spare and yet our mother protected us from the harshness of that reality with her simple, profound trust that God would provide.

This story sounds somewhat like Proverbs 30:7–9:

> Two things I ask of you, O LORD; do not refuse me before I die: Keep falsehood and lies far from me; give me neither poverty nor riches, but give me only my daily bread. Otherwise, I may have too much and disown you and say, "Who is the LORD?" Or I may become poor and steal, and so dishonor the name of my God.

This is a prayer that is realistic and has wisdom to offer.

What are the dangers pointed out in the passage if we are in a state of lack? Abundance?

⫸ UNDERSTANDING GOD'S PROMISES ⫷

To reinforce this week's promise, read the Lord's Prayer, found in Matthew 6:9–13.

The Lord's Prayer has been called "the greatest prayer of all." During Jesus' earthly ministry, He spent a significant amount of time in prayer alone, but He also prayed with His disciples and in the presence of others. The disciples asked Him, "Lord, teach us to pray" (Luke 11:1). And then He gave them this model prayer.

Through the ages, mystics and spiritual leaders have made up many definitions of prayer. Some have referred to it as simply our thoughts or our conscience. Others have called prayer "a state of mind." But prayer is much more than that—it is a two-way conversation between God and His child. In this model prayer, Jesus first addresses God as "Father" (Matthew 6:9). It's easy to gloss over this beginning, but it is so important. We are praying to the Source of all things, the One who owns all there is. This quickly positions us with the right perspective. God is our Father, and we are His child.

Much has been written about prayer, and I don't imagine any of the greats felt they ever mastered prayer. We often fail to pray simply because we have not asked like the disciples did, "Teach us to pray."

1. What has God taught you about prayer? What is mysterious, or perhaps confusing, to you about prayer?

2. In the Lord's Prayer, Jesus teaches us to pray, "Your kingdom come, your will be done" (Matthew 6:10). What does this mean in your life today?

3. There are five requests listed in the model prayer. List them here.

4. The third request is our focus in this study, "Give us today our daily bread" (v. 11). We learned in the video segment that Jesus was born in Bethlehem, a city

whose name means "house of bread." This metaphor embodies much more than food. What are your needs today? Try not to focus on what you need at the end of the week, or in a month. Focus on your needs for today.

❧ EMBRACING THE PROMISE ❧

Imagine how our Father must feel when we don't trust Him to ask for our daily bread. I've heard how children in orphanages will hide and hoard their food under their beds or pillows, because there is no promise of food for the next day. But in a normal situation any parent would be alarmed to know their child did not trust them for provision.

Review your list of needs today. Also write down the ways God has provided for you.

❧ PRAYER ❧

Pray the Lord's Prayer and fill in with your own words the needs you have. Thank God for His provision.

DAY 4

LETTING GO OF OUR WANTS

And my God will meet all your needs according
to the riches of his glory in Christ Jesus.
—Philippians 4:19

❧ RECONNECTING WITH THE PROMISE ❧

Let's begin today's lesson with further discussion on prayer. When we pray, we're free to let go of our desires that are not God's best for us. Eugene Peterson said it well: "Praying puts us at risk of getting involved in God's conditions. Be slow to pray. Praying most often doesn't get us what we want but what God wants, something quite at variance with what we conceive to be in our best interests."[1]

🔲 Think about the list of needs you wrote out in yesterday's lesson. Now finish the following statements:

"I want _____ so my life will be easier."

"I want _____ so I won't have to _____."

"I want _____ because I will be happier."

≫ UNDERSTANDING GOD'S PROMISES ≪

All of us have desires, and they may or may not be God's will for us. Because we are human, we can easily confuse our desires with our needs. When our basic needs our met, our desires can come more into focus.

Read Psalm 37:4–7.

Sometimes we hear, "Delight yourself in the LORD and he will give you the desires of your heart" (Psalm 37:4), and we think that must mean He grants us every desire we have. If that's what you're thinking, slow down and read this verse more carefully. The phrase "and he will give you the desires of your heart" is modified by "delight yourself in the LORD." In other words, our desires are fulfilled *in our delight of Him*. That is where our deepest longing is satisfied.

> The most deeply felt needs we have—for peace, for joy, for hope, for faith, for love— . . . will be met, not according to what we bring to the table, but according to the power given to Christ, which is limitless!
>
> —Shelia Walsh, *The Shelter of God's Promises* DVD

Thankfully, God does not answer our every desire. The truth is, our heart doesn't always know what is best for us. Scripture tells us that "the heart is deceitful above all things and beyond cure" (Jeremiah 17:9). But it also says it is the "wellspring" of life (Proverbs 4:23). So we have a great capacity to do both evil and good.

1. Notice the beginning words of each phrase: *delight, commit, be still*. Prayerfully read over Psalm 37 and complete a statement that reflects what your prayer to God is concerning these directives:

   I need to delight in _____.

I commit to _____.

I will be still before the Lord concerning _____.

2. Think about a desire in your life. Do you believe God is leading you toward this desire or away from it? If you are unsure, you may need more time in prayer to discern.

Read James 4:1–7.

3. Sometimes our wants can be fulfilled by opportunities that present themselves, and God allows us to exercise our free will by choosing to open or close doors. How do James's words here help us to discern if such decisions are God's will for us?

4. James admonishes us to submit to God and resist the devil (v. 7). Why do you think our desires often involve temptations from the enemy?

≫ EMBRACING THE PROMISE ≪

After completing four days of our discussion on God's provision, do you believe you are able to discern better what He desires for you to hold on to and in what areas He wants you to let go?

I'm holding on to _____.

But I'm letting go of _____.

Look back at the fill-in-the-blanks at the beginning of this day's exercises. Put a "T" by the statements that have temporal implications and an "E" by the ones with eternal implications. Does this change your perspective at all?

⇛ PRAYER ⇚

Lord, help me to completely submit to You alone. Help me to take on Your wants and desires for my life. Help me to join You in your dreams for me that are much better than my own. Help me to take delight in You and to persevere in prayer so that I may resist the devil when tempted with the wrong things. In Your strong name, amen.

DAY 5

HIS EXTRAVAGANT PROVISION

And my God will meet all your needs according
to his glorious riches in Christ Jesus.

—Philippians 4:19

⇛ RECONNECTING WITH THE PROMISE ⇚

You may remember the video segment for this week, when I shared the wild extravagance of my son, Christian's, fourth birthday.

The day of the party arrived, and the morning sun seemed to say everything would be picture perfect. The party was scheduled from 2:00 p.m. to 5:00 p.m., and at 1:30 p.m. a van pulled into our driveway. The signage on its side said Party Inflatables.

"Great choice, Barry," I said. "Christian will love this!"

Barry looked a little confused. I thought of the impending stampede of four-year-olds about to flatten our lawn. Christian ran around the yard, beside himself with excitement as he saw the giant inflatable castle take shape. William stationed himself at the front door to welcome our guests as they began to arrive, and I showed the children and their moms into the backyard.

As you recall, the doorbell kept ringing and every party service imaginable came to the door—llamas, a magician, animals, clowns, and on and on. Barry forgot to cancel all the vendors he had initially contacted for quotes.

On Christian's fourth birthday, my little family had way too much to offer, but there have been times when we feared we wouldn't have enough–enough money, time, energy, attention, enough love to go around when we all felt stretched beyond our limits.

Well, God's extravagance isn't quite like Christian's party, but God is extravagant and He sure knows how to throw parties. In this lesson, we will be reading about some of these parties.

▣ Think of a time someone treated you to grand extravagance. Did their thoughtfulness make you comfortable or uncomfortable? What was your reaction?

Parties in the Bible always seem to have an interesting twist to them. In one of Jesus' most famous parables, the prodigal son squanders his father's wealth, yet the forgiving father finds it appropriate to throw a lavish party to rejoice in his son's return. Jesus' first miracle was at the wedding in Cana, where He turned water into wine so the wedding feast could continue. Who would think Jesus would take it upon Himself to provide in this way? Was it really necessary? And when Jesus hosted a lunch party on a Galilean hillside, He fed not only his disciples but also the five thousand listening to His message—and He even provided leftovers!

> How sad it would be to never have the privilege of going to our heavenly Father to meet our needs. He has every provision we need. He loves it when we ask, when we acknowledge our need for Him in our lives.
>
> —Sheila Walsh,
> *The Shelter of God's Promises* DVD

God is sometimes difficult to figure out, but I think these illustrations show us the depth of His love for us. We are daughters of Almighty God, and He desires to give us good things, extravagant things.

Scripture reveals God's lavish promises, like these:

• "Ask and it will be given to you" (Matthew 7:7).

• "I give them eternal life, and they shall never perish" (John 10:28).

• "The prayer offered in faith will make the sick person well" (James 5:15).

How have these promises been evident in your life?

⋙ UNDERSTANDING GOD'S PROMISES ⋘

Read the story about the widow from Nain in Luke 7:11–17.

The death of a child is one of the most devastating losses I can think of as a mother. I cannot bear the thought of losing my son. God feels the same way, and when Jesus saw the funeral procession heading in His direction, extravagant love was aroused within Him. The mother, a widow, walked alone before her dead son. With this loss, she was now the poorest among poor. All her resources had been snuffed out. This time, Jesus couldn't leave her alone and helpless.

He reached out and touched the corpse, which made him unclean but shows His great compassion. What the onlooking crowd did not understand was that touching the casket did not make Christ unclean; rather, it brought God's extravagant provision to this widow and her son. Before the city gate of an insignificant town called Nain, not mentioned anywhere else in Scripture, Jesus performed a miracle of provision. Life met death and overcame it.

1. How do severe loss and hardship make room for God's extravagance?

2. Jesus doesn't act out extravagantly to impress us or to put on a show. There is always a purpose. Name the needs that were met when Jesus gave the widow back her son.

3. For this widow, her future resources were in the coffin, dead. To ask God to raise her son from the dead seems like an impossible request. What request would you like to ask God that seems too extravagant?

4. How does this promise to supply our needs tie in with the overall promise we're studying, which is that of God's shelter?

⇒ EMBRACING THE PROMISE ⇐

Read Philippians 2:6–11, a passage referred to as the *kenosis*—the emptying of Christ. He acted on behalf of humanity in a way no one could ever dream to ask of the Triune God. In my opinion, there is no better depiction of God's extravagant love in all of Scripture. Think of some practical ways you can share this extravagant love with others, and write them here.

⇒ PRAYER ⇐

Lord, You gave up Your rightful throne to come and save me from my sin. You humbled me by clothing Yourself with humanity, though You are deity. Your extravagance is unfathomable, and I praise You for loving me that much. I thank You that You not only meet my needs and refine my wants, but You answer with extravagance and give me more than I can ask or imagine. Thank You, Jesus! Amen.

THE PROMISE OF PEACE

I'M AFRAID AND FEEL ALONE

Peace I leave with you; my peace I give you. I do not give to you as the world gives. Do not let your hearts be troubled and do not be afraid.

—John 14:27

DAY 1

THE PROMISE OF PEACE

Peace I leave with you; my peace I give you.
I do not give to you as the world gives. Do not let
your hearts be troubled and do not be afraid.

—John 14:27

When we keep our focus on the solid footing of Jesus Christ, we will have peace. This isn't some fleeting feeling, but a faith in knowing who He is and that we are safely sheltered in His love and care. We must draw our peace from Him, not ourselves. How? A heart of prayer cultivates peace. When the storms of life hit, we often start a cycle of worry and fret. But when we pray, we are confronted with who He is: our shelter.

VIDEO
25 MINUTES

Watch session 3 on the Shelter of God's Promises *DVD. Keep your Bible nearby for reference and take notes in this book as needed. Fill in the blanks below as you listen to Sheila's message.*

- _____ I leave with you; my _____ I give you. I do not give to you as the _____ gives. Do not let your hearts be _____ and do not be afraid. (John 14:27)

- Jesus Christ is the _____ and _____ of all peace!

- When we keep our focus on the solid footing of _____ _____, we will have _____.

- A heart of _____ cultivates peace.

- Only Christ can _____ . . . Only He can bring _____.

- When Christ speaks to storms _____ and _____ the human heart, both obey.

KEY CONCEPTS

etaraxen (from the verb tarass):

"On your feet wear the Good News of peace to help you stand strong." (Ephesians 6:15 NCV):

MY NOTES

SMALL GROUP DISCUSSION
25 MINUTES

Break into small groups and discuss the following questions:

1. *Shalom* is the Hebrew word for "peace," meaning far more than just the absence of conflict; it refers to the peace that only God can give us. Fill out the acrostic below with words that describe what peace looks like to you. Discuss your answers (e.g., S–Safety).

   S –

   H –

   A –

   L –

   O –

   M –

2. Considering your answers to question 1, share with your group an area of your life where you are praying for peace.

No one could bind him any more, not even with a chain. For he had often been chained hand and foot, but he tore the chains apart and broke the irons on his feet. No one was strong enough to subdue him. Night and day among the tombs and in the hills he would cry out and cut himself with stones. When he saw Jesus from a distance, he ran and fell on his knees in front of him. He shouted at the top of his voice, "What do you want with me, Jesus, Son of the Most High God? Swear to God that you won't torture me!" For Jesus had said to him, "Come out of this man, you evil spirit!"

—Mark 5:3–8

3. In the video you heard the story of the man who was possessed by evil spirits. He came directly to Jesus and fell at His feet to ask for healing. On a scale of 1 to 10, how close are you walking with Jesus right now, 10 being the closest? If you feel comfortable, share your reflections with the group.

4. Some of you in the group may have had a dramatic feeling of peace when you accepted Christ as Savior. Share some of your conversion experiences together.

5. How do you keep your footing solidly on Christ in a world that's confusing and often even scary?

Bonus Question: Describe a time when Jesus miraculously brought you to a place of peace.

LOOKING DEEPER
10 MINUTES

Dig deeper into Scripture to understand the context of this promise.

The time was drawing near for Jesus to make His great sacrifice, but the disciples still didn't know the details of what would happen. He'd told them he'd be leaving, and all they could think of was life without their dear friend. The thought was nearly unbearable.

Read John 14:15–31.

Jesus knew His friends and devoted disciples were struggling with the fear of facing life without Him, so He told them He had a plan in place. They wouldn't be left alone. He would provide a Counselor who would guide them through the difficult days they'd soon be facing.

Little did they know that only with Jesus gone would they become courageous and stand boldly before the world guided by the Spirit, embodying the life of their teacher, Jesus. Only with the filling of the Spirit and the

> The good news of Christ that His disciples would share with the world, and their peace in the face of extreme opposition, was the mark that truly set them apart from the world.
>
> —Sheila Walsh, *The Shelter of God's Promises* DVD

constant challenges they would face could they possibly be transformed into confident leaders. The good news of Christ that they would share with the world, and their peace in the face of extreme opposition, would become the mark that truly set them apart from the world.

PERSONAL REFLECTION
5 MINUTES

Meditate and hear what God is teaching you through His Word and through your study group. Share your insights with the group, if you feel comfortable doing so.

Reread this week's promise of peace. Share some of your fears that you are carrying today. Then identify anything that is troubling your heart.

LIVING THE PROMISE
5 MINUTES

Discuss ways to apply what you've learned this week with your group.

Think about the fears you've been holding on to. Why do they still linger in your thoughts and heart? What can you do to give them up and welcome peace into your heart? (If you have no ideas on how to move forward, find someone who can give you good advice.)

PRAYER
5 MINUTES

Take time to pray with your group to close the session.

Pray for the person on your right and for God's peace to rule in each heart this week.

DAY 2

RUMORS OF WAR

Peace I leave with you; my peace I give you. I do not give to you as the world gives. Do not let your hearts be troubled and do not be afraid.

—**John 14:27**

⫷ RECONNECTING WITH THE PROMISE ⫸

Since the beginning of time, nations, countries, and cities have been searching for peace. Isn't that what we want when we rest our head on the pillow at night? Peace. Yet since the fall of humanity, we have lost the full realization of peace. Just when we think we've learned from our history and our past mistakes, rumors of war continue around the globe. Violence and hatred fester and grow within humanity. The Jewish Holocaust was one of the darkest hours the world has known, yet genocides continue to be a reality.

In 1994 most Americans were not aware of an atrocity that took fewer than one hundred days to accomplish. During that time close to 2 million Rwandans were killed in a conflict between the Hutu and Tutsi tribes that had been building for generations. The evil ideology was birthed from the Nazi sentiments when the Belgian colonists entered their country in the early 1920s. They saw the rich soil, the beautiful terrain of Rwanda, a place known as "the land of a thousand hills," and they wanted to take possession of it. And the way to weaken the country was to divide the people, to break down relationships.

War is probably the strongest image we have of what the absence of peace looks like. Every day journalists report fresh stories of wars tearing the fabric of innocent lives apart. Whether in the Middle East or Northern Ireland, wars are always raging around us.

🖾 If war is always a reality, what does Christ mean when He offers us His peace?

⋙ UNDERSTANDING GOD'S PROMISES ⋘

Review this week's promise: "Peace I leave with you; my peace I give you. I do not give to you as the world gives. Do not let your hearts be troubled and do not be afraid" (John 14:27).

The gospel of John differs from the other three gospels in that John is less concerned with recounting all the events that took place in Jesus' life; instead John presents a clear case for Jesus being the Son of God. He omits many of the teaching sections of the Synoptic Gospels and all of the parables found in the other books, and he includes only seven of Jesus' miracles. But he leaves out nothing that's necessary to understand the mission of Christ. The perspective of John is up close and very personal. It is the presentation of an eyewitness rather than that of a neutral observer.

John 14 shows us the disciples in the upper room with Jesus. He has just told them that He must leave them, one of them will betray Him, and Peter will deny Him. They are anxious, but Jesus tells them not to be troubled. The Greek word used for "troubled" is *etaraxen*, meaning "to stir up" or "to agitate" like water in a pool. Jesus is saying don't let your mind get stirred up with worry. He promises to send His disciples the Holy Spirit and reminds them that faith and the resulting peace that comes from a life lived trusting God are central to the believer's life.

The Jews use this blessing, "shalom," or "peace," when they greet one another or send a loved one on a journey. It means well-being, wholeness, or soundness in all aspects of life. To have shalom is to live a full, well-ordered life under God. Because Jewish people have suffered so much over the centuries, their great desire is for shalom. In the face of ruthless enemies, they have hung on to a hope built on faith. For when all of the stories have been written, all they have is hope. Their only advantage is that God truly loves them. They cling to the hope that God will prevail. Shalom is not the absence of trouble but the presence of Christ in the midst of our trouble. When we talk of peace apart from Christ, it simply means the absence of war or conflict. The great promise of Christ's peace is that even if the circumstances don't change, we can know His peace.

Jesus offers His disciples this same hope: "Peace I leave with you; my peace I give you." Jesus was leaving this earth, but He was not leaving them alone. Remember, He had just promised them the Holy Spirit. God will still be with them. This will bring peace in their hearts.

> We must draw from Him as our resource, not ourselves. A heart of prayer cultivates peace.
>
> —Sheila Walsh,
> *The Shelter of God's Promises* DVD

1. In what ways are you aware of the gift of the Spirit in your daily life?

2. John 14:26 says, "But the Counselor, the Holy Spirit, whom the Father will send in my name, will teach you all things and will remind you of everything I have said to you." Recall a time when you resisted the counsel of the Spirit. What was drawing you away from His counsel?

3. What are some practical ways we can keep pursuing peace and loving our neighbor, even when we are consumed with rumors of our ruin? Review this week's passages for further insights.

4. Have rumors of war, the economy, or current affairs taken away your level of peace in Christ? Write out your thoughts.

⁂ EMBRACING THE PROMISE ⁂

It's easy to get caught up in the stresses of our everyday lives, but God commands us, "Do not fear." To help remind you of the blessings God has given you, write out a list of the peaceful things you enjoy every day.

⁂ PRAYER ⁂

Pray for our leaders and a world in need of God's peace: Sometimes, Lord, I forget You love the whole world and died for it. I pray in times of uncertainty for those who don't know You, that they would turn to You and experience Your peace.

DAY 3

CASTING OUT FEAR

Peace I leave with you; my peace I give you. I do not give to you as the world gives. Do not let your hearts be troubled and do not be afraid.

—John 14:27

⁂ RECONNECTING WITH THE PROMISE ⁂

Throughout Scripture we read, "Do not fear." The angels often said this when they appeared among God's people. Jesus said it to His disciples multiple times. All of us have been afraid, whether of life's changes, a job promotion, a phobia, or as a result of depression. In this week's promise, we have an example of Jesus' charge, "Do not be afraid." But even when we are afraid, He is with us.

I continue to share openly about my battle with depression. I have to honestly confess that before I was diagnosed with depression, I felt tremendous fear at times. When you feel waves of despair wash over you, even as a believer, it can be terrifying. I empathize with anyone who knows what it is like to experience strong waves of despair and isolation.

A Long, Dark Night

At first I had no idea what was wrong with me. All I knew was that I felt such hopelessness and despair. It was as if someone had soaked a blanket in ice-cold water and draped it around my heart and mind. I couldn't sleep; I couldn't eat or think clearly. I would go to the ATM and not be able to remember my PIN. More than anything, there was an enduring sadness that would not lift. I didn't know what to do. I fasted and prayed and asked God to show me where I had gone wrong. How could one of God's sheep have become so lost?

I will never forget that first night as a patient in a psychiatric ward. I had never felt more alone in my life. I remember praying, "Father, if there is any mercy left in Your heart for me, please take me home. This is too hard." That first night my Bible fell open to Psalm 27:1: "The LORD is my light and my salvation—whom shall I fear? The LORD is the stronghold of my life—of whom shall I be afraid?" The truth was, however, that I was afraid of everyone and everything.

◙ Though you may not have gone through clinical depression, think about a time when despair has taken over your heart. What lies was the enemy telling you?

> For I am the LORD, your God, who takes hold of your right hand and says to you, Do not fear; I will help you.
>
> —Isaiah 41:13

Part of letting go of our fears comes from allowing them to surface. For me, I had to take time to discern why the feelings of hopelessness were taking over my heart and mind.

During that first night in the hospital, I believe that I had an encounter with an angel. I had not been aware of such an encounter before or since, but I will never forget what happened that night. I didn't get into the bed but sat in the corner on the floor with a blanket wrapped around my shoulders. I was aware of someone coming into my room about 2:00 a.m. I assumed that it was a nurse checking up on me, so I didn't even look up until I realized that the person had crossed the room and was standing at my feet. I looked up into the kindest eyes as this man placed something into my hands. It was a small stuffed animal, a lamb. He turned to leave, and as he got to the door he spoke to me. He said, "Sheila, the Shepherd knows where to find you." Then he was gone. At the darkest moment in my life, when I felt all hope was gone, I was reminded that Christ never leaves us and promises His peace through the darkest nights.

◙ Write down what you have learned to be true about God in your own dark nights. Be as honest as you can.

◙ Think of moments in your life when you felt most alone. Can you see now how God shepherded you through? How did this change your understanding of how God loves you?

> Even though I walk through the valley of the shadow of death, I will fear no evil, for you are with me; your rod and your staff, they comfort me.
>
> —Psalm 23:4

☞ UNDERSTANDING GOD'S PROMISES ☜

As a warrior and as a fugitive in his own country, King David understood fear better than anyone. His life was threatened by King Saul, then later by his own son Absalom. But David penned a beautiful psalm that communicated a sense of calm in the midst of danger. David's full attention is focused on God's presence, not his fear. He knows the answer to his fears is found in worship of Almighty God. David also understands that the only reason He can approach God is because of grace. This allows him to approach Him so darkness can be overcome.

Read Psalm 27.

This psalm was written in a "day of trouble" (v. 5), not when all was well; and probably when David was running from Saul (see 1 Samuel 22–24). The strength of King David's faith is seen in his single-minded longing for the Lord's company. Many of David's psalms recall the help of the Lord through past troubles, and he knows God will be faithful. He knows God is more steadfast than a father, more loving than any mother. He is convinced the Lord is worth waiting for. David describes the Lord in three different ways: as his light, his salvation, and the strength of his life.

1. What are some of the images of protection David uses in Psalm 27?

2. How do we dispel the darkness, according to this psalm?

> Christ promises us life here doesn't have to be this way, though. We have but to look for Him on the horizon and run to Him, ask for His peace. He can bring it with just a word, only a glance.
>
> —Sheila Walsh, *The Shelter of God's Promises* DVD

3. Everyone has been in bondage to fear at one time or another, and it can cast such an intimidating shadow over our lives, whether it is misunderstanding, physical danger, uncertainty, or even death. How has the enemy tried to make these shadows more powerful than the light of God?

4. What are some of the parts of your heart you have withheld from others, or even God, due to fear?

⫸ EMBRACING THE PROMISE ⫷

Fear can seize our hearts on many levels. Jesus knew that, and that's why we are told so many times not to fear. Insecurity. Self-loathing. Broken relationships. Shattered intimacy. All of these things can affect our confidence and trust in God.

The book of Psalms is such a rich gift to each one of us. In it we find honest expressions of the spirit, pureness of heart, and clear portrayals of emotions we all have felt. It's like David's prayer journal to God.

▨ Write out your own psalm of peace. Pray as you write it out. As David did so many times in his psalms, end with restating your confidence in God.

≫ PRAYER ≪

God, grant me Your peace as I face the temptations and stressors of my life today. Give me Your grace, that others may know Your love when they see my life, not my self-centered anxieties. I rest in Your love today and thank You for Your amazing gift of peace.

DAY 4

BLESSED ARE THE PEACEMAKERS

Peace I leave with you; my peace I give you. I do not give to you as the world gives. Do not let your hearts be troubled and do not be afraid.

—John 14:27

≫ RECONNECTING WITH THE PROMISE ≪

We know we are called to love and to love others as followers of Christ, but have you ever thought of being called to peace? Perhaps you are the one in your family who is always trying to promote an atmosphere of peace and make sure everyone is happy. You find yourself in the middle a lot—not a comfortable place to be. Middlemen get little thanks most of the time, and there is often no position more dangerous. Neither side trusts you because they know you are trying to be objective and empathize with both sides; so then you can't possibly be for them. I like what Dallas Willard says about peacemakers: "Under God's rule there is recognition that in bringing good to people who are in the wrong (as both sides usually are) you show divine family resemblance."[1] The truth is, we are all called to peace. Jesus said, "Blessed are the peacemakers" (Matthew 5:9).

The beloved pastor and theologian John Stott said, "It is hardly surprising, therefore, that the particular blessing which attaches to peacemakers is that 'they shall be called sons of God.' Peacemakers seek to do what their Father has done, love people with His love."[2] Making peace makes us children of God and by it we attest to the world that we are His offspring. Sometimes we forget we are to be bridge builders so that the kingdom of God can be realized even among those who have rejected Him.

The Roman world was looking for political and economic stability, but peace that is talked about in the Old Testament means "wholeness" and all that constitutes our well-being. Peacemakers are not simply those who bring two parties together but those actively devoted to spreading peace, reconciling the alienated.

Sometimes we are afraid of the unfamiliar. This can be the foundation of prejudices. It's easy to make critical remarks from our insecurities and ignorance, and for those of us who have grown up in the church, the blessings of a safe and secure upbringing can drive a wedge rather than serve as a resource. We think, *How can I reach out to her? I can't relate to her lifestyle.* Or *Her life is a mess, and I just don't have time to deal with that.* But the truth is that all of us are united when we come under the covering of Christ. If you don't feel an urgency to share the peace of Christ with others, you most likely have not grabbed hold of it in your own heart.

What person or people group have you shunned because of fear?

⟫ UNDERSTANDING GOD'S PROMISES ⟪

"Blessed are the peacemakers, for they will be called sons of God" (Matthew 5:9).

In the Beatitudes, found in the Sermon on the Mount, Jesus declares what the fruitful life looks like. A beatitude is a literary form found in both the Old and New Testaments that consists of a short joyful declaration like "You happy woman!"

> The word *beatitude* comes from the Latin *beatus*, meaning "happy" or "blissful."

Read Ephesians 2:14–17.

Paul wrote his letter to the Ephesians from prison. Ephesians is really a hymn of unity. Paul understood that oneness in Christ extends well beyond the church. All creation is to be brought under the headship of Christ. Unity breeds peace. Paul preached this to large crowds of people in Ephesus.

This passage clearly communicates that Christ and no one else has solved the problem of our relationship with God and with other people. Jesus is both Peace and Peacemaker.

1. As you read through the Beatitudes, you may wonder, *What does this mean for my life?* In all of them, Christ is the connecting link. What are some simple ways you can be a colaborer with Christ to bring peace to those in your church family?

2. It's easy to give up on people and relationships. To pursue peace, conflict is inevitable. What are some of the real struggles a peacemaker has to deal with?

Review the Ephesians 2 passage. The Jews believed that the Gentiles were too far away from God to be saved. Paul used the word "barrier" in verse 14 to refer to the rabbinic idea of the Law as a fence dividing Jews from other nations and races, which caused hostility. But Christ came to bring peace to all humanity.

Of whom have you ever thought, *She is too far from God?*

Paul's phrase "to reconcile" conveys the idea of restoration to an ancient unity. Christ died not just to reconcile Jews and Gentiles but also that both should be reconciled to God, and the preaching of peace has now been added through the ministry of the mission of the early church.

What kind of shoes are you wearing, and where are they taking you? Does the enemy have you believing you should be running around in fear, waiting for the next storm to blow you over? Or are your feet suited up with "the gospel of peace" (Ephesians 6:15)?

⇒⇒ EMBRACING THE PROMISE ⇐⇐

There should be no outsiders in the church family. Sometimes we marginalize people who aren't like us. Think about your church. Who do you know who is often alone or left out? Make a point to reach out to that person this week.

⇒⇒ PRAYER ⇐⇐

Take a moment to pray for the person who comes to mind.

DAY 5

THE GOSPEL OF PEACE

Peace I leave with you; my peace I give you. I do not give to you as the world gives. Do not let your hearts be troubled and do not be afraid.

—John 14:27

⇒⇒ RECONNECTING WITH THE PROMISE ⇐⇐

During this third week of study together, I pray that the peace that passes all understanding is guarding your heart. This promise of peace affects so many areas of our lives, and peace is something we can have though the storms continue to come and go in our lives.

Since the Fall, the world has been toiling, groaning for reconciliation with God. At the core of our being, sin disrupted peace because it separated us from God. God's answer to sin was His Son, Jesus Christ. No longer was humanity in perfect union with the Creator. God's solution was something so radical, so severe. Peace was accomplished through the violence of the cross.

Because Jesus overcame death, He is now with us when there are rumors of war, when relationships disappoint us and those we love even walk out on us, when the stormy waters almost overtake us. He came to cast out fear so that His peace could reign in our hearts. He came so that we too might experience the joy of what it is like to be a peacemaker. All these truths we have seen through looking at this week's promise together.

It is often so obvious we miss it: the coming of Christ changed the world, and the good news has blessed us in every area of our lives. The gospel is so simple yet so profound. Most of us are familiar with John 3:16: "For God so loved the world that he gave his one and only Son, that whoever believes in him shall not perish but have eternal life." This one truth and promise changes everything.

I believe there is a simple reason that we lose our sense of peace. It's when our focus shifts to other things. I like what Oswald Chambers said:

> A missionary is one who is wedded to the charter of his Lord and Master, he has not to proclaim his own point of view, but to proclaim the Lamb of God. It is easier to belong to a coterie [small exclusive group] which tells what Jesus Christ has done for me, easier to become a devotee to Divine healing, or to a special type of sanctification, or to the baptism of the Holy Ghost. Paul did not say—"Woe is unto me, if I do not preach what Christ has done for me," but—"Woe is unto me, if I preach not the gospel." This is the Gospel—"The Lamb of God, which taketh away the sin of the world!"[3]

We all are missionaries of the gospel when we receive Him as Savior. Chambers is admonishing us to soak in the revelation of the good news—Jesus is "the atoning sacrifice for our sins, and not only for ours, but also for the sins of the whole world" (1 John 2:2). "Atoning sacrifice" simply means "that satisfaction necessary to make us righteous before God." And because of sin, the gap was so great between the sinner and a holy God that Jesus stepped in.

Peace reigns when all eyes are on Him. Yes, it is easy to rejoice and be grateful when an answer to prayer comes or God's favor is evident. But these things are byproducts of our relationship with Jesus. What changes us, what really gives us the lasting peace of wholeness, is our salvation—the atoning sacrifice for our sins. Jesus Christ appeased the wrath of God on my behalf.

⫸ UNDERSTANDING GOD'S PROMISES ⫷

You may have made a commitment to Christ at a very early age. Or perhaps you recently accepted Jesus as Savior. No matter where we are in our relationship with God, the salvation story keeps us focused on Him.

The gift of grace is what changes our lives, not the answers to prayer or the blessings of the day. Yes, God knew we needed some encouragement on our life journey, but what really changes us is the mercy seat He has provided for us. Maybe you have shared your faith with a friend and thought, *If she would do those four steps every day like I do . . .* Our intentions can be great, but it really comes down to the one thing that has changed the world, and has changed sinners one by one: the power of the cross. The peace of God came from His sacrifice for us on the cross.

Sometimes people want to ignore the cross, the violent death that Christ suffered for us. Jesus was a sinless man, yet He endured public humiliation, floggings, starvation, and profound pain because of His pure love for us. It is hard sometimes to fix our gaze on the cross. We quickly want to take Jesus down from the cross and get to Easter Sunday, the resurrection. But it's hard to fully embrace salvation's beauty without entering into the darkness.

There is a spiritual discipline called *lectio divina*, a Latin term for "divine reading." The idea is to read Scripture prayerfully, to drink it in and ponder what the Spirit is speaking to your heart. In closing our week on this promise, I want us to bask in His Word. *Lectio divina* encourages you to stop and pray as you read. To listen. You may even find you want to sing joyfully after you finish the passage. Enter into His holy Word and let it truly nourish you.

⁂ EMBRACING THE PROMISE ⁂

Some of you may have experienced a Good Friday service that took you through the Stations of the Cross and the last week before Jesus' death. This is a shorter version to end our study. I don't want to offer any commentary on the verses. Just let the Spirit speak. You may even choose to do this exercise outside and create your own prayer walk.

Station One

Jesus Is Condemned to Death

- There is now no condemnation for those who are in Christ Jesus. (Romans 8:1)

- "God did not send his Son into the world to condemn the world, but to save the world through him." (John 3:17)

- "Whoever comes to me I will never drive away." (John 6:37)

- He was despised and rejected by men, a man of sorrows, and familiar with suffering. Like one from whom men hide their faces he was despised, and we esteemed him not. (Isaiah 53:3)

Station Two

Jesus Takes Up the Cross

- I want to know Christ and the power of his resurrection and the fellowship of sharing in his sufferings, becoming like him in his death. (Philippians 3:10)

- Now I rejoice in what was suffered for you, and I fill up in my flesh what is still lacking in regard to Christ's afflictions, for the sake of his body, which is the church. (Colossians 1:24)

Station Three

Jesus Is Stripped of His Garments

- Meanwhile we groan, longing to be clothed with our heavenly dwelling, because when we are clothed, we will not be found naked. For while we are in this tent, we groan and are burdened, because we do not wish to be unclothed but to be clothed with our heavenly dwelling, so that what is mortal may be swallowed up by life. (2 Corinthians 5:2–4)

- They stripped him and put a scarlet robe on him, and then twisted together a crown of thorns and set it on his head. They put a staff in his right hand and knelt in front of him and mocked him. "Hail, king of the Jews!" they said. They spit on him, and took the staff and struck him on the head again and again. After they had mocked him, they took off the robe and put his own clothes on him. Then they led him away to crucify him. (Matthew 27:28–31)

Station Four

Jesus Is Nailed to the Cross

- He was pierced for our transgressions, he was crushed for our iniquities; the punishment that brought us peace was upon him, and by his wounds we are healed. (Isaiah 53:5)

- We were therefore buried with him through baptism into death in order that, just as Christ was raised from the dead through the glory of the Father, we too may live a new life. (Romans 6:4)

Station Five

Life Resurrected

- "I am the resurrection and the life. He who believes in me will live, even though he dies; and whoever lives and believes in me will never die." (John 11:25–26)

- If we have been united with him like this in his death, we will certainly also be united with him in his resurrection. (Romans 6:5)

- Death has been swallowed up in victory. (1 Corinthians 15:54)

⁂ PRAYER ⁂

Close this lesson with your personal reflections and prayers and thank God for His peace.

> Whatever you have learned or received or heard from me, or seen in me—put it into practice. And the God of peace will be with you.
>
> —Philippians 4:9

THE PROMISE OF CONFIDENCE

I CAN'T SEE GOD'S PLAN IN THIS PAIN

And we know that in all things God works for
the good of those who love him, who have
been called according to his purpose.

—**Romans 8:28**

DAY 1

THE PROMISE OF CONFIDENCE

And we know that in all things God works for the good of those
who love him, who have been called according to his purpose.

—**Romans 8:28**

We say it all the time—"God's going to work this out for good." We put it on T-shirts
and bumper stickers. We remind our friends of Romans 8:28 when they get bad news,
and we put it in church bulletins and Sunday school e-mails. But do we really believe
it? Our study this week is going to get to the heart of God's desire for goodness for us,
and how that promise can give us confidence to live by faith alone, knowing that we
can always return to the shelter God provides when we face uncertainty.

VIDEO
25 MINUTES

Watch session 4 on the Shelter of God's Promises *DVD. Keep your Bible nearby for
reference and take notes in this book as needed. Fill in the blanks below as you listen to
Sheila's message.*

- And we know that in all things God _____ for the _____ of those
  who love him, who have been called according to his _____. (Romans
  8:28)

- "Everyone who drinks this water will be _____ again, but whoever drinks
  the water I give them will never _____. Indeed, the water I give them
  will become in them a spring of water welling up to _____ _____." (John
  14:14)

- Romans chapter 8 begins with "_____ _____" and ends with
  "__ _____."

- That is our calling: to be _____, to be made like Christ.

KEY CONCEPTS

dei (Greek):

kopio (Greek):

dorea (Hebrew):

MY NOTES

SMALL GROUP DISCUSSION
25 MINUTES

Break into small groups and discuss the following questions:

1. The Samaritan woman sort of stumbled into God (John 4). She did not expect Jesus to be the Savior of the world, the answer to all the baggage she was carrying with her. Identify a time in your life when you may have been running away from God or not actively pursuing Him.

2. How did God make Himself known to you in the least likely of places?

3. How did Christ's encounter with the Samaritan woman expose her life? How did He offer her shelter?

4. In the chart below, write down hardships you've faced on the left side, and across from those write the blessings that came from those experiences. Did God reveal any truth to you in this exercise? Share with the group.

Hardships	Blessings

LOOKING DEEPER
10 M I N U T E S

Dig deeper into Scripture to understand the context of this promise.

It's almost impossible to believe that God can use all things, even the terrible and shameful moments from our past (or present!), to work for good for His glory. Perhaps you embarrassed your family as a young woman and left to start a new life with no tarnished reputation. Or maybe you witnessed some horrible things no woman should ever have to see, and you've been struggling with how to deal with those memories ever since. We all have our secrets, and God knows them. He knows those embarrassing facts about us, and He loves us anyway.

Why would He do this? Why would He choose to embrace us even when we've done things that are so terribly wrong? Because it's not about us; it's about Him. What we do doesn't matter in the grand scheme of things. No one will remember them. But God's glory—that's something that will live eternally. Every man and woman on earth will one day know His glory. And that's why we can live with confidence— because God is good enough when we could never be.

PERSONAL REFLECTION
5 MINUTES

Meditate on the following question and hear what God is teaching you through His Word and through your study group. Share your insights with the group, if you feel comfortable doing so.

Romans 8 is one of the most amazing chapters of the Bible, and God's promise to work out all the twists and turns of our lives is true. Think about a situation in your life that you don't see how God could make into a good thing. Write it down and be as honest as possible. How can you trust God to fulfill His promise?

LIVING THE PROMISE
5 MINUTES

Discuss ways to apply what you've learned this week with your group.

Think about ways that you might be God's "hands and feet" to work things for good in the lives of people in your community or town. Is there something your small group can do to improve the quality of life for people near you?

PRAYER
5 MINUTES

Take time to pray with your group to close the session.

Be sure to make time to pray for one another. Pray that through this week of study, a great confidence in God will surface among your group.

DAY 2

HIS IMMANENCE

And we know that in all things God works for the good of those
who love him, who have been called according to his purpose.

—Romans 8:28

⧽⧽ RECONNECTING WITH THE PROMISE ⧼⧼

Our promise this week is an easy one to memorize. God wants to assure you that *all* things work out for good to those who love Him. I think part of the reason our hearts struggle with this promise is because the pain in our lives can be so overwhelming. The reality of pain takes over the reality of God's immanence. Sometimes it is a lot easier to believe that God is above all things (transcendent) than that He is intimately involved in all the details of our lives (immanent).

You may have heard the term *deist*. Though many Christians would say they believe God is with them, they often live out a deist mentality. A deist believes that God sort of wound up the earth and made it go but that He stays clear of our personal affairs today. This philosophy developed during the mid-eighteenth century, in the Enlightenment. It was a distortion of Christianity, negating a personal relationship with Christ. "The universe is fully capable of moving without God's intervention," said the philosophers of the day.

One of the mysteries of the Christian life is that it seems God does hide from us from time to time. No matter how much we pray or try to listen, it seems we get silence. Whether God gives you a pillar of fire to guide you in the dark seasons or not, the truth is that He is there even when you feel He has forgotten you.

▨ Think of a time or a season you endured when you could not trace God's hand in your life, when it seemed almost like He abandoned you.

⧽⧽ UNDERSTANDING GOD'S PROMISES ⧼⧼

We know the outpouring of the Holy Spirit assured the fledgling body of Christ that God was with them, ever present, doing miracles by the power of His Spirit. But this was also true in the Old Testament. He was faithful to keep watch over His people and also reveal His immanence.

Read Genesis 15:12–17.

God was talking to Abram clearly in this passage, and His immanence caused Abram to trust Him. Later, God changed Abram's name, which suggests a new intimacy with him. He changed his name from Abram to Abraham, and the name of his wife, Sarai, to Sarah. The new name, Abraham, means "father of a multitude"; but there was a deeper meaning in the change. The letter *h* that was added to Abram's name and to his wife's was from the Lord's own name Jehovah, and it was a sign that Abraham and Sarah were to be His children, to obey Him, and as far as they could, to be like Him.

- In verse 17, a blazing torch appeared in the dark before Abram. How has God made Himself known to you when you felt like you were in the dark?

- A covenant is a promise made between God and man. How does this covenant communicate the nearness of God?

Read Genesis 32:22–30.

Prior to his wrestling with God that night, Jacob was dealing with hatred toward his brother. The last time he saw his brother, Esau, he threatened to kill him. Earlier in this chapter, angels came to Jacob, also signifying the nearness of God, telling Jacob about his brother (see Genesis 32:1–21).

Jacob survived wrestling with God, but developed a limp. He survived being face-to-face with God. *Peniel* means "face to face" (v. 30).

- There are many more examples of God's immanence throughout Scripture, so we know this is how God has cooperated with His people since the beginning. What reminders do you have or memories of when God came near and made Himself known to you in a specific way?

Jacob wrestled all night with God. He persevered. Where in your life do you need to develop more persistence? How does God's immanence help us persevere?

> Many places in the Bible, God gives new names to His people. He changed Jacob's name to *Israel*, which means "he struggles with God."

✺ EMBRACING THE PROMISE ✺

Review the promises of God we've learned so far, and meditate on the desires God has for you. Write them down in a place you look frequently, whether it's your phone, wallet, refrigerator, or desk. Review them regularly and let them remind you that your confidence is built on the foundation of Christ.

✺ PRAYER ✺

Lord, it is easy to misplace our confidence in something other than You. We say today we are confident that You are working all things out for our good and that You are nearer to us than we can fathom. In Your great name, amen.

DAY 3

REFINE ME

And we know that in all things God works for the good of those
who love him, who have been called according to his purpose.

—Romans 8:28

✺ RECONNECTING WITH THE PROMISE ✺

Often we miss out on some of the blessing of Romans 8:28 because we reject God's loving discipline. The refining process is apart of the Christian life, and it is the very process God uses to make us more like Jesus. When we reject His correction, we will be inclined to miss the truth of Romans 8:28. God is much more than a security blanket; He is the great "refiner" (see Malachi 3:2–3).

We've been called "according to his purpose"—not toward our own purposes. And to be fit for our calling, sometimes the refining process is the best method to grant us the courage we need to go where He wants us to go or the strength to stay in the place we are. Read the following excerpt from L. B. Cowman's work, *Streams in the Desert*:

> Around the turn of the twentieth century, a bar of steel was worth about $5. Yet when forged into horseshoes, it was worth $10; when made into needles, its value was $350; when used to make small pocketknife blades, its worth was $32,000; when made into springs for watches, its value increased to $250,000. What a pounding the steel bar had to endure to be worth this much! But the more it was shaped, hammered, put through fire, beaten, pounded, and polished, the greater its value.
>
> May we use this analogy as a reminder to be still, silent, and long-suffering, for it is those who suffer the most who yield the most. And it is through pain that God gets the most out of us, for His glory and for the blessing of others.[1]

Sometimes it is hard to determine if the cause of temporal suffering is from our own decision or from God's discipline of us. No matter the source, God can use it as a means to mold us to reflect more of His image.

▣ Take a moment to think about some of the great men and women in the Bible: Abraham, Noah, Paul, and Job. You may have a favorite Bible character. Choose one to look up in your Bible and trace the refining process in his or her life.

> Now that we know what we have—Jesus, this great High Priest with ready access to God—let's not let it slip through our fingers. We don't have a priest who is out of touch with our reality. He's been through weakness and testing, experienced it all—all but the sin. So let's walk right up to him and get what he is so ready to give. Take the mercy, accept the help.
>
> —Hebrews 4:14–16 MSG

⫸ UNDERSTANDING GOD'S PROMISES ⫷

Shortly after Jesus promised the disciples that the Holy Spirit would be their constant guide and comforter in life, He tells them a story centered on principles of gardening.

Read John 15:1–16.

In this passage, Jesus gives His followers, us, a distinct warning: If you drift away from Me, you will be cut off. Useless branches that bear no fruit will be burned in the pruning fire. But for those who do love Christ and are dedicated to His message, God will hold them close. Not only will they remain in Him, but they will become more fruitful as a result. In this passage, once again, we are reminded that we are safe in Jesus; He is our shelter.

1. In the Greek, *prune* means "to cleanse." What branches in your life has God cut off? How did you discern it was God doing the pruning and not just consequences of poor choices?

2. Jesus says to His disciples, "Remain in me, and I will remain in you" (John 15:4). *The Message* renders this verse, "Live in me. Make your home in me just as I do in you." What do you think it means to "remain in" Jesus?

3. God can use even our poor choices to refine us, as we see in the promise this week—all things work together for good. How is this evident in your own regrets?

> My son, do not despise the LORD's discipline and do not resent his rebuke, because the LORD disciplines those he loves, as a father the son he delights in.
> —Proverbs 3:11–12

4. Think about a godly person in your life whom you admire. How does this person testify to John 15:8, "This is to my Father's glory, that you bear much fruit, showing yourselves to be my disciples"?

≫ EMBRACING THE PROMISE ≪

Reflect on God's discipline in your life. Are you resisting Him in the process or have you submitted to it? Explain.

> No discipline seems pleasant at the time, but painful. Later on, however, it produces a harvest of righteousness and peace for those who have been trained by it.
> —Hebrews 12:11

≫ PRAYER ≪

Lord, thank You that you love Your children and You desire for us to bear much fruit in our lives. Help me not to resist what is good for me and what will bring more glory to You.

As you continue to pray, ask God what will specifically bring Him glory in your life.

DAY 4

HIS REMARKABLE FOLLOW-THROUGH

And we know that in all things God works for the good of those
who love him, who have been called according to his purpose.

—Romans 8:28

≫ RECONNECTING WITH THE PROMISE ≪

This week's promise should be sinking deeper and deeper into our hearts. To reinforce this powerful promise, read Philippians 1:6: "being confident of this, that he who began a good work in you will carry it on to completion until the day of Christ Jesus."

There is no one with follow-through like Jesus. He promises to complete what He started, and He will. At the point of crisis, sometimes life's shattered dreams try to convince us that there is no way God can use the broken pieces for good.

Complete the sentences below by recording a hardship you faced and the resulting blessing that came out of that difficult time.

• During my childhood (or young adult years), _____ .

  I'm grateful for the good that came from _____ .

• During my marriage (or dating relationship), I struggled with _____ .

  I'm grateful now to see the good that came from _____ .

⟫ UNDERSTANDING GOD'S PROMISES ⟪

Read John 8:1–11.

The religious leaders, if you can imagine, put the adulterous woman on display as an outcast. In verses 4 and 5, we see their religious, hardened hearts exposed as they ask Jesus, "Teacher, this woman was caught in the act of adultery. In the Law Moses commanded us to stone such women. Now what do you say?"

They did not care about this woman, her story, where she had been. She was worthless to them—they were just using her as a way to trap Jesus with a trick question. In essence, she was a commodity to build up the Pharisees' platform of religiosity.

In response to the religious leaders' question, Jesus began writing in the dirt. We don't know what He wrote, but scholars have speculated. I don't know what Jesus wrote, but this is sort of my guess. He knew how despised this woman was and how much more righteous the Pharisees believed they were than this woman. So I wonder if Jesus was writing things like, *What about you, religious leader—were you one of the men who slept with this woman?* Or was He writing the names in the sand of all the men in the crowd who had slept with her?

Sometimes it is our shame that keeps us from believing God can work out the worst times for our good. We think, *Well, even if He can, I don't deserve it.* After reading this story, answer the following questions:

1. How did Jesus restore the adulterous woman's life?

2. Though this woman was living a life of sin, God showed her great mercy. From this passage, what attitudes from the Pharisees can we detect regarding how they viewed this woman?

3. Most of us regret something we've done to a friend, a family member, or even to ourselves. Take a moment to determine if this personal regret has caused a wedge between you and God. How do you now perceive that God could use this for good in your life?

4. Take a moment to list all the thoughts that make you doubt God can use your story for His good and His glory. Are there some behaviors He is asking you to change? Is He asking you to forgive yourself? Be prayerful about your response.

> The tremendous promise that "all things will work together for good to those who love him, who have been called according to his purpose," is found in one of the most glorious chapters in the whole New Testament. Romans chapter 8 begins with "no condemnation" and ends with "no separation." Paul explained that because of what Christ has done for us, we stand righteous in the sight of God; and because of God's great love for us, nothing in heaven or earth can come between us.
>
> —Sheila Walsh, *The Shelter of God's Promises* DVD

The Message translation of Hebrews 4:14–16 reads: "Now that we know what we have—Jesus, this great High Priest with ready access to God—let's not let it slip through our fingers. We don't have a priest who is out of touch with our reality. He's been through weakness and testing, experienced it all—all but the sin. So let's walk right up to him and get what he is so ready to give. Take the mercy, accept the help."

➤➤ EMBRACING THE PROMISE ⫷⫷

"Let us then approach the throne of grace with confidence, so that we may receive mercy and find grace to help us in our time of need" (Hebrews 4:16).

Hebrews 4:16 says we can approach God with confidence. Sometimes our confidence is misplaced in our "good deeds" or our "work" or our "appearance." We do not have a God who is out of touch with our reality. Like the adulterous woman, perhaps you feel rejected by your own faith community due to judgment and others not caring about your pain. He wants you to come to Him and receive all He has for you. We are cowriters with Him of our life story. He is the Creator who can provide those unwritten pages we long to write. Perhaps you are waiting to offer forgiveness to someone, or perhaps you are waiting for someone to approach you.

In light of our study today, begin to see the good God is doing in your life. Complete the blanks below with your own insights:

▣ Today, though I wish _____, I know God can _____.

➤➤ PRAYER ⫷⫷

Heavenly Father, thank You for the extravagant gift of Your love to us, and for Your desire to give us a good life. Help me understand what "good" means in the language of heaven, and give me the ability to make life better for my family, friends, and community for Your glory.

DAY 5

GOD IS IN CONTROL

And we know that in all things God works for the good of those who love him, who have been called according to his purpose.

—Romans 8:28

➤➤ RECONNECTING WITH THE PROMISE ⫷⫷

I pray this week has been one of great encouragement and has helped you though the unexpected circumstances of each day. As we close out this week, I want to focus on one of the most assuring realities about our God: His sovereignty. This is a truth the Bible teaches in tension with our free will and has led to the debate of various camps of Christianity throughout the existence of the church. But for today's lesson, we will be looking at God's divine intervention in our human affairs, stressing the point that at the end of the day, we aren't in control—God is. There should be a freedom in our hearts when we realize humanity is not sovereign. No one is sovereign. Only God.

> **God's sovereignty:** the biblical teaching that God is King, Supreme Ruler, and Lawgiver of the entire universe.

John Calvin, the great sixteenth-century Reformer, said he was "arrested" by God. His life was on another path, pursuing his father's dream for him—a career in law—but then God took him in a different direction, toward the church. He wrote of times in his life when God's intervention was positively overriding the circumstances or situation. Calvin said, "God by a sudden conversion subdued and brought my mind to a teachable frame."[2] For Calvin, this illustrated the sovereign rule God had over his life. He read Scriptures through the grid of God being the source of all that is and ever was. Much of Christendom has been influenced by John Calvin's writings. As believers, we can trust in God's sovereign rule that sustains all His creation and guides us for the ultimate purpose that all things might glorify God alone.

Several of God's names express His sovereignty.

Genesis 14:18–20—*El Elyon* means God Most High

Exodus 6:3—*El Shaddai* means God Almighty

Genesis 15:2; Deuteronomy 3:24—*Adonai Yahweh* means Lord God

What confidence can be gained in these names of God? Write out your thoughts.

God's sovereignty is expressed to humanity in His comprehensive plan carefully and lovingly laid out for the world. In other words, He works out everything in conformity with the purpose of His will (see Ephesians 1:11).

It's one of the great challenges of our faith to hold these two truths at the same time: God is loving and God is powerful. You may be tempted to think, *Why would a loving God allow bad things to happen? Is He loving but not powerful enough to intervene? Or is He powerful but not loving enough to intervene?* In 1 Corinthians 13:12, the apostle Paul wrote that on this earth we see as in a glass darkly, but one day we will see face-to-face. Until then, we rest in His sovereign power and love.

⁂ UNDERSTANDING GOD'S PROMISES ⁂

We're going to do something a little different today and look at a progression of verses that will bring us to a significant truth about this week's promise. Let's start with Hebrews 1:3:

> The Son is the radiance of God's glory and the exact representation of his being, sustaining all things by his powerful word. After he had provided purification for sins, he sat down at the right hand of the Majesty in heaven.

▣ Circle the descriptions about Christ and underline the actions Christ takes in this passage.

The Greek word translated "sustaining" in Hebrews 1:3 is *phero*, which means to "carry" or "bear." This definition does not mean simply "sustain" but has an active sense of purposeful control.

> A man's steps are directed by the LORD. How then can anyone understand his own way?
>
> —Proverbs 20:24

▣ According to Hebrews 1:3, what is Jesus carrying (or upholding)?

This isn't the only place in Scripture where we see that Jesus sustains us. Take a look at Colossians 1:17:

> He is before all things, and in him all things hold together.

▣ This passage says that in Jesus, "all things hold together." Make a list below of some of the things Jesus is holding. (Examples include creation, our physical bodies, the circumstances of our lives, governments and world politics, etc.)

▣ If Jesus were not holding all things together, what would happen?

Not only are humans sustained by God, but all of creation submits to His will.

Praise the LORD from the earth, you great sea creatures and all ocean depths, lightning and hail, snow and clouds, stormy winds that do his bidding. (Psalm 148:8–9)

▣ What obeys God's command, according to this passage?

Finally, we are told that even the kings of the earth bow to God's sovereign goodness.

At the end of that time, I, Nebuchadnezzar, raised my eyes toward heaven, and my sanity was restored. Then I praised the Most High; I honored and glorified him who lives forever. His dominion is an eternal dominion; his kingdom endures from generation to generation. All the peoples of the earth are regarded as nothing. He does as he pleases with the powers of heaven and the peoples of the earth. No one can hold back his hand or say to him: "What have you done?" (Daniel 4:34–35)

1. How did God restore the king's sanity?

2. What people or things try to compete with God's sovereignty to dethrone His power in our modern culture?

3. When have you lived out a situation in your life as if you were sovereign and not God?

> In him we live and move and have our being.
> —Acts 17:28

⇛ EMBRACING THE PROMISE ⇚

Have you pondered the truth that God is in charge of our successes and failures? All our circumstances are working according to His plan. All of our talents and abilities are from the Lord. Paul asks the Corinthians, "What do you have that you did not receive? And if you did receive it, why do you boast as though you did not?" (1 Corinthians 4:7). Think about how God is indeed working all things out for your good because you love Him. What talents and abilities can you thank Him for and surrender fully to Him at this moment? Be as specific as you can.

⇛ PRAYER ⇚

Lord, I thank You for your sovereign rule and that I alone do not have to make my life be successful. You are laboring with me, and You have given me all the good gifts I need to glorify You through my life. In Your sovereign name, amen.

THE PROMISE OF LOVE

I DON'T BELIEVE THAT ANYONE COULD REALLY LOVE ME

For I am convinced that neither death nor life, neither angels nor demons, neither the present nor the future, nor any powers, neither height nor depth, nor anything else in all creation, will be able to separate us from the love of God that is in Christ Jesus our Lord.

—Romans 8:38–39

DAY 1

THE PROMISE OF LOVE

For I am convinced that neither death nor life, neither angels nor
demons, neither the present nor the future, nor any powers, neither
height nor depth, nor anything else in all creation, will be able to
separate us from the love of God that is in Christ Jesus our Lord.

—Romans 8:38–39

God loves us for keeps and tells us, *I belong to you and you belong to Me forever.* What
a comfort that declaration is for every moment you feel wounded, cast away, unloved,
or unwanted. What peace and joy that brings to the life that has been shunned. A
promise like that could make a lonely, despairing soul dare to reach out to the world
again. A promise like that shatters walls of isolation and ushers in enough love to be
passed around.

VIDEO

25 MINUTES

Watch session 5 on the Shelter of God's Promises *DVD. Keep your Bible nearby for
reference and take notes in this book as needed. Fill in the blanks below as you listen to
Sheila's message.*

🎬 For I am _____ that neither _____ nor _____, neither _____
nor _____, neither the _____ nor the _____, nor any _____,
neither height nor depth, nor anything else in all creation, will be able to separate us from the love of God that is in Christ Jesus our Lord. (Romans
8:38–39)

> If we feel that we are still in hiding, there remain places in our souls that have
> not been opened to His light and life.
> —Sheila Walsh, *The Shelter of God's Promises* DVD

- Shame tells us not that we've _____ something wrong but that we _____ something wrong.

- Nothing can _____ us from the love of God. Nothing—not _____ or _____ or _____.

- When the pain of _____ _____ _____ is greater than the pain of _____, then you will change.

- God's love conquered both _____ and _____.

KEY CONCEPTS

mastigos (Greek):

kraspedon (Greek):

sozo (Greek):

MY NOTES

Touching even the hem of Jesus' robe, which is what she did, was no small thing. It meant a huge risk for this woman. Under Old Testament Law: "When a woman has a discharge of blood for many days at a time other than her monthly period or has a discharge that continues beyond her period, she will be unclean as long as she has the discharge, just as in the days of her period. Any bed she lies on while her discharge continues will be unclean, as is her bed during her monthly period, and anything she sits on will be unclean, as during her period. Whoever touches them will be unclean; he must wash his clothes and bathe with water, and he will be unclean till evening" (Leviticus 15:25–27).

—Sheila Walsh, *The Shelter of God's Promises*, chapter 5

SMALL GROUP DISCUSSION
25 MINUTES

Break into small groups and discuss the following questions:

1. Discuss some of the desperate circumstances that the woman described in the video segment faced.

2. The woman, knowing what had happened to her, came and fell at Jesus' feet. Trembling with fear, she told Him the whole truth. How does God use the truth to heal us?

3. Guilt tells us we have *done* something wrong; shame tells us we *are* something wrong. Are you more plagued by guilt or by shame?

4. Most of us have felt unlovable. When we are convinced we are unlovable, how does this distance us from God's love?

LOOKING DEEPER
10 MINUTES

Dig deeper into Scripture to understand the context of this promise.

God has promised us His love. It is an eternal, unending love that is pure and holy in every way. But we have no concept of this in our earthly relationships. Even the most perfect couple has their petty quarrels and their minor frustrations. No one is immune from the sin that invades life on earth.

So when the relationships we share with other people leave us feeling wounded, frustrated, hurt, or angry, we can take shelter in God's perfect love. This love fills us with peace and joy. It enables us to minister to others with humility and compassion. It inspires us to serve our families without complaint. When we live knowing no matter what we do or say, God will love us, our lives open up in freedom and the possibilities for spreading His love to the world seem endless.

PERSONAL REFLECTION
5 MINUTES

Meditate and hear what God is teaching you through His Word and through your study group. Share your insights with the group, if you feel comfortable doing so.

There is nothing more the enemy would like you to believe than that you can be separated from God's love. This week's promise is one of the most comforting passages in all of Scripture. Sometimes when we face illness, punishment, discouragement, or shame, we think God has stopped loving us. But that's totally untrue: His love protects us and shelters us forever.

Describe a time when you've felt unloved by God, and then recall the ways that He's provided emotional shelter during the storms of your heart.

LIVING THE PROMISE
5 MINUTES

Discuss ways to apply what you've learned this week with your group.

When life is a struggle for us, it's hard to remember that God loves us unconditionally and forever. Ask someone you know and trust to be that voice of encouragement in your life, and you in theirs. Commit to meeting together and praying for one another regularly.

PRAYER
5 MINUTES

Take time to pray with your group to close the session.

Pray for one another, and read aloud Romans 8:28–29 over those in your group.

DAY 2

THE POWER OF LOVE

For I am convinced that neither death nor life, neither angels nor
demons, neither the present nor the future, nor any powers, neither
height nor depth, nor anything else in all creation, will be able to
separate us from the love of God that is in Christ Jesus our Lord.

—Romans 8:38–39

⫸ RECONNECTING WITH THE PROMISE ⫷

In his book *The Four Loves*, C. S. Lewis explores the nature of love. Lewis was studying John, who wrote, "God is love" (1 John 4:16). In his study, he found the idea of
love is often more complicated than we think at first glance. *Love* is a term we hear as
a casual expression of endearment—as in "I love that recipe"—and in contrast, it is
a word reserved for the sacred moments of life, as in wedding vows—"I promise to
love . . . till death do us part."

Lewis looks at the four Greek words for love, representing affection, friendship,
romantic love, and charity. Affection (*storge*) describes the feelings we have for those
we are familiar with. It is a forgiving expression of love and can overlook character,
as often family does. It's the most natural of relationships. Friendship (*phileo*) is a
second kind of love that goes beyond a superficial friendship to sharing a common
bond, mutual interests, and admiration for one another. Eros (*eros*) is romantic love,
which captures the passion between two people in love, but is often what Hollywood
exploits, giving its viewers a skewed understanding of what love really should look
like. Charity (*agape*) is what Lewis called the highest form of love, love that is unconditional. It is a Christian understanding of how God loves us. All other forms of love
are subordinate to this supreme, unconditional love.

God warns us that love can become perverted (see Proverbs 7) because we can
make it be something that it is not, even an idol when it isn't under the lordship of
Christ. Ignatius, the first-century bishop of Antioch, described *eros* as something to
be shattered. He was being taken to Rome to be martyred and implored the Roman
Christians to let him die for the sake of Christ. He declared that his passionate love
for the world, his desire, had been crucified with Christ and he had found happiness

in the incorruptible love of God.[1] *Eros* is bigger than merely romantic desire; it is anything that focuses on self-gratification. This kind of love in itself isn't evil, but it has the power to overtake our lives and impair our judgment. It professes to fulfill us with all happiness. Enough is never enough. The Bible doesn't mention *eros*, so we will focus on *agape*, which is mentioned in 1 John 4:16 to describe God Himself.

▣ What are some common fallacies we assume about love?

▣ Write down the name of a friend who has been a faithful companion, who has loved you with the bond of friendship (*phileo*).

> *Agape*: love revealed in Jesus Christ.

≫ UNDERSTANDING GOD'S PROMISES ≪

Read Romans 8:31–39.

While the epistle to the Romans is focused on condemnation and righteousness, in it we also learn that the emphasis should not be on our attempting to keep the Law, expecting it to bring about good outcomes. Rather, we should trust God to work things for our good because of the righteousness we have in Christ. This is *agape* love.

In Romans 8:38–39, Paul lists the things that cannot separate us from the love of God. Of course, the love spoken of here is the mercy that makes us righteous before God's holy justice. Nothing can tear us away from His mercy and bring us back under the condemnation of the Law. So the *love of God* equals our shelter and security in the imputed righteousness we receive from Jesus.

> And I pray that you, being rooted and established in love, may have power, together with all the saints, to grasp how wide and long and high and deep is the love of Christ, and to know this love that surpasses knowledge—that you may be filled to the measure of all the fullness of God.
>
> —Ephesians 3:17–19

The interesting part of these two verses is the list of adversaries. Paul begins with "neither death nor life" (v. 38). It is unexpected that he would use a negative conjunction to introduce life, but Paul is emphasizing the suffering that believers were facing, dying for their love for Christ. No matter how hard things are, even death cannot separate us from our promised eternal life.

Next come "angels" and "demons" (v. 38). Once again angels are not necessarily positive. *Angel* literally means "messenger" or "intermediary." Genesis 6 is a discussion of angels that have fallen, and in Job we have the adversarial conversation between Satan and God. So Paul could be talking about those who rule on earth and those from the heavens who are standing against God's purposes.

Then Paul inserts the dimension of time: "neither the present nor the future" (v. 38). Neither the confrontations of today nor those that are yet to come—a possible allusion to the end times—present a challenge to God.

Next, the mention of "neither height nor depth" (v. 39) implies once again that no supernatural power from above or below can challenge the power of God. Nothing that God created can separate us from Him. Paul has covered everything, everywhere. Nothing that we have faced or anything that we could possibly face will separate us from God's love and righteousness.

1. Have you ever stopped to think about the fact that because of God's love for you, your righteousness can never be taken away? When have you pushed away from God because you didn't feel worthy of His love?

2. Think about a relationship in your life that was not healthy. How did this expression of love fall short of what you thought it promised?

3. In recent weeks, what has God been speaking to you specifically about His love for you?

> He loves us for keeps and tells us: *I belong to you and you belong to Me forever.*
>
> —Sheila Walsh, *The Shelter of God's Promises* DVD

≫ EMBRACING THE PROMISE ≪

I love how this passage reads in *The Message* translation:

> So, what do you think? With God on our side like this, how can we lose? If God didn't hesitate to put everything on the line for us, embracing our condition and exposing himself to the worst by sending his own Son, is there anything else he wouldn't gladly and freely do for us? And who would dare tangle with God by messing with one of God's chosen? Who would dare even to point a finger? The One who died for us—who was raised to life for us!—is in the presence of God at this very moment sticking up for us. Do you think anyone is going to be able to drive a wedge between us and Christ's love for us? There is no way! Not trouble, not hard times, not hatred, not hunger, not homelessness, not bullying threats, not backstabbing, not even the worst sins listed in Scripture:
>
> *They kill us in cold blood because they hate you.*
> *We're sitting ducks; they pick us off one by one.*
>
> None of this fazes us because Jesus loves us. I'm absolutely convinced that nothing—nothing living or dead, angelic or demonic, today or tomorrow, high or low, thinkable or unthinkable—absolutely *nothing* can get between us and God's love because of the way that Jesus our Master has embraced us. (Romans 8:31–39 MSG)

What has allowed you to believe that God doesn't really love you that much? Maybe you think that God loves others, but He doesn't love you because . . . Try to put a word to the root of the problem (i.e., self-esteem, shame, hardships, etc.). As you answer, reread the promise and remember the power of His love.

≫ PRAYER ≪

Lord, there are many things in this life that try to tear me away from You. Thank You for Your love that endures forever. Thank You for Your extravagant love. No matter what tomorrow brings me, there is no power greater than the love You have for me, Your child. Help me to grasp this in a deeper way this week.

DAY 3

WHAT ABOUT ME?

For I am convinced that neither death nor life, neither angels nor demons, neither the present nor the future, nor any powers, neither height nor depth, nor anything else in all creation, will be able to separate us from the love of God that is in Christ Jesus our Lord.

—Romans 8:38–39

⟫ RECONNECTING WITH THE PROMISE ⟪

Being overlooked and underappreciated is what wives, mothers, and daughters experience from time to time. Perhaps you work harder than anyone in the workplace, and your hard work was overlooked recently—even worse, someone else got the credit for it! Or perhaps, as you go about your day, you wonder if anyone in your family knows there were twenty-three tasks on your to-do list that had to be accomplished to keep the household running smoothly. Maybe you wish your husband would notice the worry on your face and reach out to you with a comforting hug. You flop into bed and wonder, *God, do You see? Can You show me evidence of Your love for me?*

I think sometimes it is especially hard for women to realize we cannot earn God's love because our days are so full of doing, and we often don't know how to receive love and support from others. Rate yourself below on your ability to receive from others, 1 being the lowest and 10 being the highest. Then rate yourself when it comes to receiving from God. Note if the two scales correlate or not. Note your observations.

My ability to accept help from others

1	2	3	4	5	6	7	8	9	10
(lowest)									(highest)

My ability to accept help from God

1	2	3	4	5	6	7	8	9	10
(lowest)									(highest)

⋙ UNDERSTANDING GOD'S PROMISES ⋘

On day 1 of this week, we focused on the hemorrhaging woman in Mark 5. In the midst of this story of healing, Jairus was also petitioning Jesus for help. Note the different touches of healing He administers to those He loves.

Read Mark 5:21–43.

Jairus was desperate. His "little daughter" was dying (v. 23). Can you just hear the affection in his voice and see the pain in his eyes? Jairus's little daughter, the joy of his life, lay sick. He knew his only hope was Jesus. He rushed to the shore, pushed his way through the crowd, and fell at Jesus' feet. "Come and put your hands on her," he begged, "so that she will be healed and live" (v. 23). Jesus immediately recognized Jairus's faith and agreed to help him, but on their way He was held up by a woman who also needed Him. Can you imagine Jairus—wringing his hands, looking over his shoulder to see if anyone was sending word from his home? *Come on, Jesus*, he must have been thinking. *You can help her later; my daughter might not make it.* But Jesus took his time with the woman, and Jairus was patient.

Then, the sight he feared most: a messenger from his home. The man slowed his pace as he saw Jairus, and he dropped his head in reverence. *No need to bother the teacher any more. Your baby . . . she's gone.* My guess is that Jairus fell to his knees, sobbing. The pain that overtook his heart was unbearable. But Jesus saw what was happening, and He knows the pain of a Father losing His only Son. He walked to Jairus, knelt beside him, put His hand on his shoulder, and said, "Don't be afraid; just believe" (v. 36).

What a beautiful picture of compassion. Jesus healed Jairus's daughter that day, and the family would never forget how the love of God radically changed their lives forever.

1. Jesus went back across the Sea of Galilee, probably at Capernaum. Jairus was the elected leader of the local synagogue, so he had close ties to the Pharisees. How did he respond to Jesus in verses 22 and 23? Why was this a risky thing to do? What did Jairus ask Jesus to do?

2. Jesus raised the girl from the dead, but He only allowed the girl's father and mother and three disciples to be present. Taking her hand, He said, "Little girl, I say to you, get up!" (v. 41). Think about a time God conveyed to you, *I'm here*, in a way only He would know. Was it through a certain scripture, the timing of a friend's visit? Explain.

3. Sometimes it is easy to question God's timing and mistakenly think His delay means that God has forgotten you. Describe a time this has been true for you.

4. The messenger announced that Jairus's daughter was dead and said, "It's no use bothering the teacher now." When have you given up on God's love too soon, only to find He was there all along?

⇛ EMBRACING THE PROMISE ⇚

Jairus's daughter was only allowed to struggle for a short time before Christ healed her, but the hemorrhaging woman had to wait twelve years. How is Jesus' love clearly revealed in both stories?

His love for us has the power to heal. God has not overlooked you. Perhaps you have not taken time to ask Him, but think of an emotional or physical pain that you want Jesus to heal. You may or may not have shared it with anyone before. Write it out on paper. Will you commit to trusting God to heal you?

⁂ PRAYER ⁂

Lord, sometimes we do not ask You for healing or a display of Your love because we feel unworthy of Your time. But You show us that You love all Your children with the same powerful love. Thank You for the stories of love and healing in Your Word. Help me be open to receive the full expression of Your love for me today. In Your loving name, amen.

DAY 4

LOVING GOD

For I am convinced that neither death nor life, neither angels nor demons, neither the present nor the future, nor any powers, neither height nor depth, nor anything else in all creation, will be able to separate us from the love of God that is in Christ Jesus our Lord.

—Romans 8:38–39

⁂ RECONNECTING WITH THE PROMISE ⁂

Jesus' response to the disciples when they asked, "Teacher, which is the greatest commandment in the Law?" was "Love the Lord your God with all your heart and with all your soul and with all your mind" (Matthew 22:36–37).

As we learn to embrace God's love in our lives, we then can start to reflect the life of discipleship as we learn to love Him with our whole being. What does a life devoted to loving God with all our heart, soul, and mind look like? I believe when we are resolved to do just that, our life takes on greater dimension and greater meaning. When we begin to give our whole self to God, He has a way of showing us a better plan, a better way for our life. And sometimes it is one we never could have dreamed of on our own.

Take a moment to reflect on which part of this commandment is easiest for you. Is it easier to love God with your heart or your mind? What does it look like to love God with your soul?

⟫ UNDERSTANDING GOD'S PROMISES ⟪

Read Deuteronomy 6:4–5, also referred to as the Shema, the central prayer in the Jewish prayer book. Jesus restates this to His disciples in the New Testament:

> Hear, O Israel: The LORD our God, the LORD is one. Love the LORD your God with all your heart and with all your soul and with all your strength. (Deuteronomy 6:4–5)

What matters most is the love that links God and people together. Though we think of the Law sometimes as legalistic, it was impossible for the Israelites to obey the Law without loving God, as the Law was also concerned with the heart.

The Shema is not suggesting that we love God partly with our heart, partly with our mind, and so on, as much as it is saying we love God with everything—our whole self.

1. Read the following verses and put them into your own words:

   Psalm 119:11:

   Philippians 4:8:

   Deuteronomy 11:1:

2. How does the Shema reflect the intimate love of the covenant relationship we have with God?

3. What are some of the things we withhold from God in our heart?

4. To love God with our soul indicates a willingness to lay down even life itself for God. What part of your life do you think you have held up to God with a clenched fist?

5. Loving God with our might or strength can be translated as our "resources." Think about someone you know who may need a resource you have, whether it is financial or practical help. What can you do to better love God with your resources this week?

> I wonder if it takes facing the worst of all we believe to be true about ourselves, whether right or wrong, to be able to embrace the love of God at the very depth of our beings. If we feel that we are still in hiding, there remain places in our souls that have not been opened to His light and life. God wants more for us. He wants us to know that there is nothing in heaven or earth, no power or person, no pain or shame that can separate us from His love.
>
> —Sheila Walsh, *The Shelter of God's Promises* DVD

⫸ EMBRACING THE PROMISE ⫷

The Psalms speak over and over about the enduring love of God. Just when we think we've exhausted His love toward us, He is faithful to remind us His love has no limits. Write down the ways God's love has been limitless to you. How can you show His limitless love to others who don't know about it?

⫸ PRAYER ⫷

Read Psalm 136 as your closing prayer. Speak it aloud with a heart of gratitude.

DAY 5

LOVING OTHERS

For I am convinced that neither death nor life, neither angels nor demons, neither the present nor the future, nor any powers, neither height nor depth, nor anything else in all creation, will be able to separate us from the love of God that is in Christ Jesus our Lord.

—Romans 8:38–39

⫸ RECONNECTING WITH THE PROMISE ⫷

Try to write out this week's promise from memory. I hope that this week of focusing on God's love has made you more aware of how much He does love you. There is so much to ponder when we think about His love for us, but we have at least laid a groundwork to build on in the weeks to come. What we are capable of as recipients of His love is remarkable. If we each felt compelled to serve God because we love Him, what a force that would be in our world today! God's love can take away pain, feed hungry children, serve a local hospice, and comfort the marginalized.

Paul said, "Christ's love compels us" to act (2 Corinthians 5:14).

▨ During this week of study, how has God's love impacted how you love others around you? Has it been easier to be patient, kind, forgiving?

⫸ UNDERSTANDING GOD'S PROMISES ⫷

Read Matthew 22:39 and John 13:34–35.

Because we hear about the need to love one another so often, it can go in one ear and out the other. How easy it is for us to forget the mandate to love others as ourselves and exalt temporary things as a way to avoid people. Jesus even said the way people will know we are His disciples, that we are His family, is how we love others (John 13:35).

But when we get tired or busy or frustrated, we often live like the end justifies the means. In other words, it doesn't matter how we get that worship service planned, who we offend, or if we have to walk over others—the end justifies the means. But in the life of the church, that never works. Relationships mean everything to God, and love is the only fruit that remains. In the famous love chapter, 1 Corinthians 13, Paul admonishes believers to become perfect in love. The Greek word for "perfect" is *teleios*—which means having arrived or being "mature."

The Pharisees were often caught up in looking the part of being "religious," so much so that they often forgot to love those around them, like tax collectors, prostitutes, and lepers. Their self-imposed religious laws kept them from following the second greatest commandment: "Love your neighbor as yourself" (Matthew 22:39).

1. Have you been afraid to love someone who may be considered to be outside your circle of community?

2. When was the last time you received unexpected, lavish love from a friend? How did this impact you?

In my own life, when I know I've let go of my fears and let God lead, I've experienced a grace I can't even explain. Just when I've convinced myself that someone's pain is too dark and that I can't look, I've found God is right there, changing me and showing me how to love that person with the power of God.

3. What dark corner have you been avoiding? If the Spirit is leading you to reach out to someone in particular, write it down here.

4. In light of this week's promise, have you ever thought of people separating you from the love of God? How can people try to keep us from the love of God?

❧ EMBRACING THE PROMISE ❦

Probably one of the most famous works of Western art is Michelangelo's monumental *The Creation of Adam*, which adorns the ceiling of the Sistine Chapel. God touches fingers with Adam, and God and man are united. We've put this image on coffee mugs and stationery, framed it in our hallways, and even used it in cartoons. But undeniably when tourists look up and view it, the reaction is "Bravo!" as they marvel at the beauty and the artist's message of truth.

God entered the dark world through Jesus, His Son, because He loved us, not because He needed us. In 1 John 4, John writes, "This is how God showed his love among us: He sent his one and only Son into the world" (v. 9). When you look at Michelangelo's masterpiece, you can feel what the artist felt: life flows from God's hand to Adam. His love gives us life. God's life-giving love, then, is the theme of this passage.

John continues on, telling us He is the source of all love:

Dear friends, let us love one another, for love comes from God. Everyone who loves has been born of God and knows God. Whoever does not love does not know God, because God is love. . . . Dear friends, since God so loved us, we also ought to love one another. No one has ever seen God; but if we love one another, God lives in us and his love is made complete in us. (1 John 4:7–8, 11–12)

Post these verses somewhere you'll see them frequently, and read them whenever you're feeling unsure of God's love for you.

❧ PRAYER ❦

Bow and silently thank God that He is a God of love. Just sit with a heightened awareness of Him and His unwavering love for you. Listen to what He might be speaking to you during this time. Pray that you would let go of anything that you've made to be the unpardonable sin; ask God for help to forgive yourself. Then pray for God to show you specifically where He might be calling you to take His love after completing this lesson.

Go today grounded in the promise of His love.

If something I'm asked to do for another feels burdensome;
If, yielding to an inward unwillingness, I avoid doing it,
Then I know nothing of Calvary love.
If the praise of man elates me and his blame depresses me;
If I cannot rest under misunderstanding without defending myself;
If I love to be loved more than to love,
Then I know nothing of Calvary love.
If the burden my Lord asks me to bear be not the burden of my heart's choice,
And I fret inwardly and do not welcome His will,
Then I know nothing of Calvary love.
If I covet anyplace on earth but the dust at the foot of the cross,
Then I know nothing of Calvary love.

—Amy Carmichael

THE PROMISE OF GRACE

I HAVE FAILED

My grace is sufficient for you, for my power is made perfect in weakness.

—2 Corinthians 12:9

DAY 1

THE PROMISE OF GRACE

My grace is sufficient for you, for my power
is made perfect in weakness.

—2 Corinthians 12:9

Grace can be a difficult concept to grasp, because it is hard to believe God loves all of us equally and to understand that His grace shelters us regardless of what we do or leave undone. Probably because there are no other relationships on earth like that! We're all impacted by what we do and say; there are consequences and rewards in our earthly relationships. But when God sees us, He only sees the redemptive work of His Son. There is nothing *we* need to do to earn God's favor; it's already been done for us by the only One who could do it—Jesus.

VIDEO

25 MINUTES

Watch session 6 on the Shelter of God's Promises *DVD. Keep your Bible nearby for reference and take notes in this book as needed. Fill in the blanks below as you listen to Sheila's message.*

- 🎞 My _____ is sufficient for you, for my _____ is made perfect in _____. (2 Corinthians 12:9)

- 🎞 If we allow _____ to occupy our hearts we force _____ right out the back door.

- 🎞 When you look closer at the Greek word for "shame," it actually means, "____ _____."

- 🎞 "My grace is sufficient" means "_____ _____, ____ _____ _____ _____."

KEY CONCEPTS

charis (Greek):

"For the grace of God that brings salvation has appeared to all men." (Titus 2:11 NKJV):

MY NOTES

> We were created in His image, in His likeness. And the enemy wants to mar that and make us believe otherwise. He wants to keep us in a state of shame. He wants to disfigure our faces, so that what others see is shame.
>
> —Sheila Walsh,
> *The Shelter of God's Promises* DVD

SMALL GROUP DISCUSSION
25 MINUTES

Break into small groups and discuss the following questions:
Keep your Bibles open to Acts 9, the story of Saul's conversion.

1. How do we see profound grace exhibited in the testimony of the apostle Paul?

2. What parts of Paul's testimony can you relate to in your own story of grace?

3. The video segment cautions us that shame and grace cannot share a room. Have you found this to be true in your own life? Why do you think it is so easy to hang on to our shame?

It is hard to believe that God loves each of us equally, without measure or merit, and that His grace shelters us regardless of what we do or leave undone. I think it's so hard because there is no other relationship on earth like that. Every other relationship we have is affected, to some extent, by how we behave and what we say.

—Sheila Walsh, *The Shelter of God's Promises* DVD

Bonus Question: Think of a recent time in your life when, in your eyes, you failed. Did you encounter God's unexpected grace in the midst of the struggle?

 LOOKING DEEPER

10 MINUTES

Dig deeper into Scripture to understand the context of this promise.

The word *grace* can mean various things. When we pray before a meal, we say "grace," offering thanks. If someone is kind toward us, we acknowledge their "graciousness." In light of Scripture, grace can refer to different aspects of our faith. There is "common" grace and "divine" grace. Common grace is something all of humanity benefits from, like the order of Creation. Divine grace is the saving work of Christ, which for our purposes in this study we will call *sufficient grace* (2 Corinthians 12:9).

The word *grace* is used 156 times in the New Testament. It is derived from the Greek word *charis*, which denotes "goodwill," "sweetness," and "loving-kindness." This cultural understanding of the word existed as far back as Homer's epic poetry, dating around the eighth century BC. But in the New Testament, the word takes on deeper meaning relating to redemption. It's understood to mean that God grants favor on behalf of sinners who don't deserve it. And grace is available to all of humanity who receive it, as we read in Titus 2:11, "For the grace of God that brings salvation has appeared to all men."

 ## PERSONAL REFLECTION
5 MINUTES

Meditate on the following question and hear what God is teaching you through His Word and through your study group. Share your insights with the group, if you feel comfortable doing so.

Sufficient grace is what Paul experienced on the road to Damascus. When were you first confronted with God's sufficient grace?

 ## LIVING THE PROMISE
5 MINUTES

Discuss ways to apply what you've learned this week with your group.

Sometimes it is easy to take for granted even the common grace in our daily existence. Write down evidences you can see in your day of God's common grace. All of us know someone who is in need of God's sufficient or saving grace. Write down in the margin the name of someone you are praying for who does not know Christ. Be faithful to pray for this person throughout your week of study.

 ## PRAYER
5 MINUTES

Take time to pray with your group to close the session.

Heavenly Father, Your grace washes over me and makes me new every morning, but sometimes I forget You give me this amazing gift. Make me aware, hourly, minute by minute, of the blessings of Your grace. Change my life, that others may see Your grace evident in me.

DAY 2

MORE THAN SUFFICIENT

My grace is sufficient for you, for my power
is made perfect in weakness.

—2 Corinthians 12:9

⇒》 RECONNECTING WITH THE PROMISE 《⇐

This week's promise proclaims to us, "His grace is sufficient." Those who draw near to Jesus and accept this gift are fully and completely saved from all sin and condemnation. The cross is the only place where we find complete forgiveness, reconciliation, and strength to make it through the unimaginable.

But I think we would be remiss to forget how even Christians fall into the trap of wondering, *Is God's grace enough, even for this?* We may not even realize it, but our rejection of God's perfect gift can actually be an attitude of arrogance, not humility.

Cindy's Story

The news story was shocking. A pastor, Fred Winters, had been standing in front of his congregation in a small church in Maryville, Illinois, when a gunman walked down the aisle toward him and shot him in the chest. Fred used his Bible to try to protect himself from the first bullet, which sent paper cascading into the air like confetti. Church members would later say that they thought it was part of a skit, a sermon illustration. In many ways it was, but not as they imagined. It became the greatest sermon illustration for those who knew and loved Fred and his wife, Cindy, on the breadth, depth, and width of God's grace to hold you when everything you understand comes crashing down around you.

Cindy and their two daughters were not at the 8:15 service that morning, but as Cindy drove up to second service it was clear that something was very wrong. Fred Winters had been preaching a sermon on what true happiness is, declaring that it is rooted and grounded in Christ and not in our circumstances. That was about to be put to the test for a mom, two young daughters, and a grieving church.

When we look at the pain in life, sometimes it is overwhelming to think of God's grace being enough for the worst moments imaginable. But that is the promise. When everything around you falls away, God still shelters you.

⫷ UNDERSTANDING GOD'S PROMISES ⫸

Read 2 Corinthians 12:7–10.

This small portion of 2 Corinthians is one of the most difficult in the New Testament to interpret. Paul speaks of a particular difficulty that has been given to him to temper his pride. He tells of a "thorn in the flesh" (*skolops te sarki*) and a "messenger of Satan." *Skolops* means something that is sharp and pointed, which could denote anything from a fishhook to a stake. Some commentators speculate the thorn to be opponents of Paul, a relational hardship. The Greek text literally reads "an angel of Satan strikes me," so they tie the messenger or angel to the suffering that Paul experienced. Others see the two as unconnected hardships—speculating that God supplied the thorn to keep Paul humble while Satan separately tormented him.

Possible physical ailments that have been suggested include speech problems, running sores in the eyes, epilepsy, and various nervous disorders. Some wonder if it was sexual temptation. But many believe it could have been chronic malaria, as this was a common illness in the Mediterranean. Whatever the source, Paul focuses on the good of the gospel as God gave him the grace and strength to bear the hardship. It is clear from this passage that Paul was privy to amazing revelations that most will not see until heaven. This thorn kept Paul wholly dependent on God while he was on this earth.

Verse 9 is a powerful statement about how the grace of God can turn any burden into a source of renewal and a conduit for victory. Jesus is saying to Paul that His grace is enough to surpass the most challenging of opponents. He is saying that Paul's weakness and suffering would be a place where His grace would shine. For the power of Jesus' grace is only fully apparent when shown against the background of extreme suffering. Without trials and suffering we cannot see the greatness of God's mercy. But in the face of any problem or disappointment or chronic suffering, the grace of Jesus is more than enough to turn a setback into victory. In verse 10, Paul says that in his weakness he is truly strong.

Paul suffered greatly at the hands of his opponents: imprisonment, beatings, stoning, and other abuses that at times brought him close to death. The thorn in the flesh seems to be something that was constant rather than an intermittent oppression.

But in all this, Paul was content in his life. He actually took some pride in his hardship. For this is where Christ was glorified. And the promise to us is that no matter what the problem is, grace is greater. This was the promise of Christ to Paul and it is the promise of God to us. His grace is more than enough. Our role is to recognize His grace; our suffering becomes a tapestry where the glory of Christ is revealed in us.

1. How has God used the suffering in your life to highlight His grace?

2. Whether Satan was the culprit or not, we do know that God was responsible for the negative answer to Paul's request. Think of a time when you asked for a certain affliction to leave you, but it lingered. What grace did God work out in your life that you see now in hindsight?

3. Why do you think we do not have a more specific description of Paul's "thorn in [his] flesh" (v. 7)?

For it is by grace you have been saved, through faith— and this not from yourselves, it is the gift of God—not by works, so that no one can boast. For we are God's workmanship, created in Christ Jesus to do good works, which God prepared in advance for us to do.
—Ephesians 2:8–9

Cindy's Story, continued

I want to look again at a part of Cindy's story that reveals how the glory of our God shines in our darkest night.

I had the unique privilege of meeting Cindy and her daughters in the summer of 2010, just a few short weeks after the first anniversary of Fred's death. Through our publisher, Thomas Nelson, the Women of Faith team asked women across the country to nominate someone who showed a deep trust in God in the worst moment of her life. Cindy was nominated, and it was clear to all involved that her story should be told. So I flew to Maryville, Illinois, with a film crew to meet this family. I don't know what I expected, but I know what I was a little afraid of. I was afraid that the pressure on Cindy to be a "good witness" for Christ would rob her of the freedom to tell the truth about her pain. But within the first ten minutes of meeting this beautiful woman, any fears I had were dispelled. Hopefully someday Cindy will write her own story, but let me simply say this: As I looked into the eyes of this young woman who walked through the valley of the shadow of death, I saw one who found the Shepherd of her soul to be more than enough. She did not airbrush the pain, which was palpable, but the grace of God exhibited in her life was staggering.

⫸ EMBRACING THE PROMISE ⫷

This is the crux of orthodox Christianity—grace. No other worldview or religious system is founded on a personal relationship with God that is based on loving grace. However, within Christianity, we can fall prey to a life or a system of good works, just as the Pharisees did.

Can you see this tendency in your own faith tradition? Explain.

⫸ PRAYER ⫷

Lord, thank You for the unmerited favor we have with You. Lord, when we don't even know what we need, You know. Through the circumstances of this week, I know Your grace will be more than sufficient. In Jesus' name, amen.

DAY 3

GRACE ISN'T CHEAP

My grace is sufficient for you, for my power

is made perfect in weakness.

—2 Corinthians 12:9

⫸ RECONNECTING WITH THE PROMISE ⫷

We've emphasized that grace is truly a gift from God. We can do nothing to be worthy of the gift of salvation. Yet, as students of Scripture, we have to interpret Scripture in light of Scripture.

You may be familiar with German theologian Dietrich Bonhoeffer. One of his most famous books, *The Cost of Discipleship*, addresses what he calls "cheap grace." Bonhoeffer says:

> Cheap grace means the justification of sin without the justification of the sinner. Grace alone does everything they say, and so everything can remain as it was before. "All for sin could not atone." Well, then, let the Christian live like the rest of the world, let him model himself on the world's standards in every sphere of life, and not presumptuously aspire to live a different life under grace from his old life under sin.[1]

From the gospel story, we know that the price of our salvation was costly—it wasn't cheap. Yet sometimes we forget our need to turn from our own selfish desires and repent.

▣ Cheap grace is something we often offer ourselves, as in, *Well, if I do this, God will forgive me anyway, so what's the big deal?* How does this attitude cheapen God's grace in our lives?

⇛ UNDERSTANDING GOD'S PROMISES ⇚

Cindy's Story, continued

If you were to sit down with Cindy Winters today, you would see two things as clearly as I did about grace.

1. Grace is God's heart of love toward us
2. Grace is God's heart of love working in us.

You may be tempted to question how Cindy experienced the goodwill of God toward her. She lost her husband, and her daughters lost their father. But what I saw as I sat with her is that it is one thing to claim that Jesus is the Good Shepherd when times are good; it is quite another when you find you cannot stand and His staff is the only thing that holds you strong. The psalmist David wrote in Psalm 23:4, "Even though I walk through the valley of the shadow of death, I will fear no evil." For there to be a shadow, there has to be light. Even in our darkest nights, the Lamb of God is with us.

Grace is also the goodwill of God working in us. We took a break in our filming schedule for lunch, and Cindy suggested a local barbecue restaurant. Before we had a chance to order our meal, the waitress sat down with Cindy and poured out her story. In her brokenness, Cindy had become a conduit of the love and grace of God to others.

This woman's story was very different from Cindy's in that she was the one who had wounded another. I listened as Cindy shared that grace is not only for those who have been wounded but also for those who wound others.

Read Romans 6:1–7.

Paul knew from experience what we do to justify our sins, so he asked the rhetorical question, "Shall we go on sinning so that grace may increase?"

Such a mentality would fit with Bonhoeffer's definition of cheap grace.

Cheap grace is the grace we bestow on ourselves. Cheap grace is the preaching of forgiveness without requiring repentance, baptism without church discipline, Communion without confession. . . . Cheap grace is grace without discipleship, grace without the cross, grace without Jesus Christ, living and incarnate.[2]

1. The truth is, all sin is covered under the saving power of the cross. He will forgive us, even when we choose to go our own way. However, we will suffer the consequences of our choices. What consequences have you had to deal with due to poor choices?

Read Romans 6:12–18.

2. In this passage, Paul uses the metaphor of slavery to refer to sin. When we are a slave to sin, what does our life look like? How does it impact our heart and attitude?

> For sin shall not be your master, because you are not under law, but under grace.
> —Romans 6:14

3. When we are in the grip of God's grace, sin no longer controls us or has power. Can you point to a pivotal time in your life when this proved to be true?

4. Paul says a new life becomes a slave to righteousness. What does verse 18 mean?

≫ EMBRACING THE PROMISE ≪

In the video segment, I shared my grandmother's favorite hymn, "Rock of Ages":

Nothing in my hands I bring,
Simply to Thy cross I cling.
Naked, come to Thee for dress,
Helpless, look to Thee for grace.

Take a moment and read this week's promise. Sometimes our baggage is what keeps us from believing God's grace is sufficient. Read each line of the hymn and confess the ways you may have forgotten the cost of grace.

- *Nothing in my hands I bring.* Lord, I'm sorry I have carried _____ that has kept me from Your grace.

- *Simply to Thy cross I cling.* Lord, I'm sorry I have clung to _____ instead of to You.

- *Naked, come to Thee for dress.* Lord, I have covered my shame with _____.

- *Helpless, look to Thee for grace.* Lord, I look to You for grace.

⫸ PRAYER ⫷

Lord, sometimes we aren't even aware of the ways we try to work out our own salvation without Your grace. I confess my helplessness to You and know that Your grace is more than enough. The price You paid for my soul was costly. May I be a testimony of grace to others. In Jesus' name, amen.

DAY 4

FREEDOM TO FAIL

My grace is sufficient for you, for my power
is made perfect in weakness.

—2 Corinthians 12:9

⫸ RECONNECTING WITH THE PROMISE ⫷

God is always the initiator of love and mercy—of the kind of strength that fills in our weaknesses, the kind of perfection that covers our flaws, and the kind of shelter that says, "I'm going to keep you and love you through all your failings." God is the one who pursues us, woos us to this place of grace, the shelter of His promises.

My thirteen-year-old son has defined this kind of grace as "forgiveness." When I asked him to explain, he said, "Well, when you think that He is God and we are not, there is no reason for Him to keep loving us when we mess up. But He does. He forgives us. That is grace."

Yes, that is grace.

Where we mess up, He mends it. Where we are weak, He is strong. Where we have no control over our imperfections, He rushes in to touch us and lovingly shows us the way He sees us and calls us to be. He patiently listens to our doubts and fears and proclaims, *With all My heart, I'm telling you that you are loved just the same on the days when you feel you've done a good job and on the days when you know you have blown it. You are loved and always will be loved, and I am going to love you and forgive you to the very end.*

You may be someone who has grown up in the church and you have let a secret life keep you from the grace of God because you have feared rejection. Remember God has forgiven you. In this lesson, I pray that God softens your heart toward yourself, toward your own failures.

> One of the hardest things to do as women is to remember the need to forgive ourselves for past failures. Are you still condemning yourself for something in your past? If not, explain how you overcame your feelings of guilt.

⋙ UNDERSTANDING GOD'S PROMISES ⋘

Perhaps as you look at your life today you feel that you are not worthy of God's grace. That is the whole point of grace—not one of us is worthy. It is God's extravagant gift to everyone who will receive it.

Read the parable of the wedding banquet, found in Matthew 22:1–14.

When Jesus was asked why He spoke to the people in parables so often, He said in effect that there were two reasons: (1) to instruct His followers and (2) to conceal God's kingdom until it was time for it to be revealed. In other words, parables served to reveal and to conceal. The parables Jesus shared in Scripture are stories with layers of truth that the Spirit can help us unravel. The parable of the wedding banquet, like all other parables, offers various messages to the reader.

When studying a parable, I think it is always good to list questions as you read the text. After reading it a couple of times, you may be amazed at how many questions you can answer from further reflection.

1. Who is the king in the parable? Who is the son? And who are the invited guests?

2. What do the wedding garments represent in this story? (See Isaiah 64:6 and Isaiah 61:10.)

3. Have any failures kept you from receiving His garments of grace?

> God made him who had no sin to be sin for us, so that in him we might become the righteousness of God.
>
> —2 Corinthians 5:21

4. If you were to put on the garment of grace for good and never take it off for the rest of your life, how would this impact the relationships around you?

❦ EMBRACING THE PROMISE ❦

As you read the parable of the wedding banquet, you may be tempted to ask, "What if I am not one of the chosen?" In his commentary on this text, Matthew Henry writes, "It is not owing to God that sinners perish, but to themselves—whoever will, let him come."[3] Grace is not only a gift, but it is also our responsibility to receive it and become more like Christ.

Romans 3:23 says, "For all have sinned and fall short of the glory of God." Yet we struggle to let go and to lay our defeats and failures at the foot of the cross. Perhaps we wear the wedding garments for a day, only to take them off again. Or we lay our failure at Jesus' feet only to take matters into our own hands and try to hide our failures.

Thank God we do not have to pay the debt of what we owe. His grace can cover all our failures. Think for a moment about your own child. If you do not have a child, think of your childhood. Did you allow your child to fail? Were you allowed to fail? There is a strength that comes when we get back up again and realize that our failures cannot defeat us—they only make us stronger.

In the space below, name your failure and read over the Scriptures from our study today. What is God speaking to you about your failures now?

⫸ PRAYER ⫷

Take time to examine your heart to determine whether you harbor unforgiveness toward yourself. Remember also to be mindful of the person you are praying for this week, that he or she might receive the gift of grace.

DAY 5

THE PARADOX OF THE CROSS

My grace is sufficient for you, for my power
is made perfect in weakness.

—2 Corinthians 12:9

⫸ RECONNECTING WITH THE PROMISE ⫷

The promise of grace is like a diamond. It has many facets, and if you hold it up to the light at different angles, there is a fresh beauty to behold. We have looked at some of the truths about grace together, but we have only begun to scratch the surface of this great gift. We know that there is a common grace that is upholding the created order, and we know there is a saving grace that God desires for all humanity to receive. When we forget to respond to God's grace with a humble and repentant heart, we can end up trampling on the lavish gift God has extended to us and making it a commodity to be consumed rather than a gift of sacrifice. And as we find the balance of truth in our lives, God wants us to know that when we fail, He is right there ready to pick us up.

To close our week, I want to look at the paradox of the cross. We've mentioned that part of the reason it is so hard to simply receive God's grace in its purity is because we have no other relationship quite like our relationship with God. Grace is what makes the cross a symbol of forgiveness, not shame. Grace took the helplessness of God on the cross, the emptying of Himself, and gave us eternal life. His death gave us life.

Sometimes we look at various scriptures and, at a glance, they seem to contradict one another, but Scripture does not go against itself. Rather, our faith is full of paradoxes—seemingly contradictory statements. Paul was able to boast in His weakness, because He understood the paradox of the cross. It is when we are weakest that we are strong in Christ. The world has set us up to boast in our strengths, but Paul understood that even our strengths can be weaknesses that keep us from leaning on God for our every breath.

▨ Think for a moment about the strengths God has given you. Now your weaknesses. List a few of each. Which are easier for you to think about?

⫸ UNDERSTANDING GOD'S PROMISES ⫷

Read John 19:23–30.

It is hard to think about grace coming to the world through the violence of the cross. Jesus suffered in agony and emptied Himself of any rights, though He could have called on legions of angels. But He submitted to His Father's will. Paul understood the power of submission. His boasting in weakness wasn't a mind game where he was just supposed to accept oppression and defeat passively. Rather, God revealed to him that a divine power dwells within human weakness. Now that is grace! Our lack just makes more room for God to take over.

1. In human terms, how did the cross translate to utter defeat?

2. What were Jesus' last words on the cross?

3. Paradoxically, from God's perspective, how is the cross a symbol of victory and life?

Read 2 Corinthians 11:29–30.

It's tempting to ask God for miracles and great displays of His power in our lives that show He is with us and loves us, but the kingdom of God is no sideshow or three-ring circus. God is glorified when in our weakness we lean on His strength.

4. Have you ever thought about God being more interested in your weaknesses than your strengths? How does God use our weaknesses to bring Him glory?

5. Grace does not start with us, but it starts with God. Jesus took action when we were helpless, without any ability to help ourselves. How has this truth been evident in your own life?

6. Think about a circumstance right now in your life where you know your resources are not enough. You know you are going to need God's grace to suffer through the pain or difficulty. In this space, begin to boast in your weakness. Name what you lack with boldness and present your weaknesses unashamedly before God.

⇛ EMBRACING THE PROMISE ⇚

Grace doesn't tell us that our bad choices or failures don't matter; quite the reverse. Grace tells us that our failures expose us for who we really are, which puts us in a right posture toward God to receive from Him.

As we close our discussion on the promise of grace, take a moment to review your notes, new insights that you don't want to forget, and write out the aspects of grace you have grasped in a deeper way. Perhaps the Spirit has shown you something that you never knew before. How has this study allowed you to receive more of His grace? Write your thoughts on God's grace here:

⁂ PRAYER ⁂

God, thank You for the promise of grace that has surrounded me when I wasn't even aware. Thank You for the power of the cross. Though the cross was a symbol of defeat, Jesus conquered death, and because of His grace, I am victorious.

Conclude your prayer time conversing with God about the person you committed to pray for.

> The shelter of the cross casts its shadow over our broken hearts and welcomes us home.
> —Sheila Walsh, *The Shelter of God's Promises* DVD

THE PROMISE OF HOPE

I'M BROKEN

God has said, "Never will I leave you; never will I forsake you." So we say with confidence, "The Lord is my helper; I will not be afraid. What can man do to me?"

—Hebrews 13:5–6

DAY 1

THE PROMISE OF HOPE

God has said, "Never will I leave you; never will I forsake
you." So we say with confidence, "The Lord is my helper;
I will not be afraid. What can man do to me?"

—**Hebrews 13:5–6**

Let's face it; life is hard. We're tempted to lose faith when trials come our way, and so often we are bombarded with news of tragic and frightening things happening in the lives of our friends, family, and community. When this happens we often feel alone. But God offers us a ray of light in the darkness. We can hold tight to His promise of hope, knowing that even though in this world we will struggle and have trials, we can take heart because he is the Lord of our hearts.

How does God's promise never to leave us or forsake us—to be our helper—fit into this picture?

VIDEO
25 MINUTES

Watch session 7 on the Shelter of God's Promises *DVD. Keep your Bible nearby for reference and take notes in this book as needed. Fill in the blanks below as you listen to Sheila's message.*

- Never will I _____ you; never will I _____ you." So we say with confidence, "The Lord is my _____; I will not be afraid. (Hebrews 13:5–6)

- One of the most _____ elements of our suffering is the _____ and _____ we're able to share with others when they suffer too.

- Our experiences with pain and struggle, trouble, and hardship do not _____ the promises of God at all.

- He calls us to live with questions draped in _____.

KEY CONCEPTS

Mary Magdalene:

"My God, my God, why have you forsaken me?" (Psalm 22 NIV):

Rabboni:

MY NOTES

> As she wept, she bent over to look into the tomb and saw two angels in white, seated where Jesus' body had been, one at the head and the other at the foot. They asked her, "Woman, why are you crying?"
> —John 20:11–13

SMALL GROUP DISCUSSION
25 MINUTES

Break into small groups and discuss the following questions:

1. Choose the statement that best describes where you are:

   - "I know God is real, but I don't have a firm hold of His hope in my life."

   - "I believe God is working everything out for my good, but I'm struggling from day to day to hang on to hope."

   - "Because of a recent trial, God has blessed me with His comfort and I know I wouldn't have the hope I have now without persevering through it."

2. Suffering and comfort go hand in hand, as we see illustrated in the story of Mary Magdalene and Jesus. How has your own suffering opened a door for you to comfort someone else?

3. This week's promise reminds us of the fact that God will never leave us—His presence is constant. Because we forget His presence, we often find ourselves misplacing our hope in temporal things. If that is true for you, what does that look like? Where do you tend to turn for hope when you forget to turn to God?

4. Take a moment to review the promises we've studied so far. Try to recall each verse that correlates with the promise.

   1. The Promise of Jesus

   2. The Promise of Provision

   3. The Promise of Peace

   4. The Promise of Confidence

   5. The Promise of Love

   6. The Promise of Grace

Bonus Question: How do all of these provide a source of hope, all pointing to Jesus, our Source?

LOOKING DEEPER
10 MINUTES

Dig deeper into Scripture to understand the context of this promise.

Read Psalm 22:1–3.

Throughout the Psalms, the psalmists often state their emotions and honest feelings unashamedly before God, but then their thoughts turn back to the truth about God, a *yet* statement. In this psalm, we see that as David cries out to God. He feels that God has forsaken him and left him alone. All day and all night he calls for

God's help, but he doesn't feel God's presence nearby. *Yet* he knows God is on His throne. He knows Israel praises Him.

Christ quoted this verse when He was on the cross, moments before He died. He too felt alone and was in anguish, but, like David, Jesus knew that God was on His throne. His power was set

> Our experiences with pain and struggle, trouble and hardship do not diminish the promises of God at all.
>
> —Sheila Walsh, *The Shelter of God's Promises* DVD

firm, so he had hope. He knew He could trust God and His plan. He didn't need to fear, and neither do we. God will never leave us—even when we don't feel He's nearby, He's watching over us and we can praise Him for His power.

PERSONAL REFLECTION
5 MINUTES

Meditate on the following question and hear what God is teaching you through His Word and through your study group. Share your insights with the group, if you feel comfortable doing so.

Have you ever been in a place so dark that you felt as if you were all alone? Describe the situation and how God pulled you toward His hope.

LIVING THE PROMISE
5 MINUTES

Discuss ways to apply what you've learned this week with your group.

What experiences in your life have given you hope? How can you have more of those experiences in your life?

PRAYER
5 MINUTES

Take time to pray with your group to close the session.

Lord, open up our hearts to receive Your hope. Remind us that You've given us a future and it is bright with Your glory. Send us divine encounters with others who will speak Your hope into our lives, and vice versa. Let us live with an attitude of hopeful expectation, not grumpy cynicism, so that others may see Your joy in us.

DAY 2

HOPE IN MY HELPER

God has said, "Never will I leave you; never will I forsake
you." So we say with confidence, "The Lord is my helper;
I will not be afraid. What can man do to me?"

—Hebrews 13:5–6

⟫ RECONNECTING WITH THE PROMISE ⟪

Most of us would agree that we could all use a little extra help, whether it is around
the house, on the job, or with our children. I don't think I know anyone who is *not*
busy. We all seem to have our plates full, even overloaded. Sometimes it feels like
life is never going to slow down and the days keep rolling by, with or without us.
Sometimes we don't even stop to ask for help because we are so used to just taking
care of everything ourselves.

The second part of our promise this week says, "The Lord is my helper; I will
not be afraid. What can man do to me?" (v. 6) Sometimes the most effective prayer
we can pray is simply, "Please, God, help me." I believe He is faithful to answer this
prayer every time.

▨ When is the last time you asked God to help you?

⟫ UNDERSTANDING GOD'S PROMISES ⟪

Our promise is from the book of Hebrews, the only book of its kind in the New
Testament. It stands alone without association with an individual author or a specific
church as its audience. We know from the content that the readers were most likely
Jewish or under the influence of those church leaders who were working to pull the
church back into the Jewish faith.

The first nine chapters of Hebrews are rooted in the Jewish tradition and give a Jewish apologetic or reasoned argument for accepting Jesus as the ultimate High Priest. At the beginning of chapter 10, we learn that the Jewish law is really just a partial truth. It is called a "shadow" of what Christ brings to the faith (v. 1). From verse 19 on, the author leaves the theological discussion and offers an application of the new covenant. We are told to enter the holy place with confidence and to draw near with a sincere heart with full faith. Faith now becomes the focus of the book.

Chapter 11 is totally devoted to demonstrating the faith of the past heroes of Israel; and chapter 12 tells us to "fix our eyes on Jesus, the author and perfecter of our faith" (v. 2).

The last chapter, where we find the promise of hope, describes the character of one who is a disciple of the great High Priest. The author calls us not to be drawn into the world with its immorality and love of money. Instead we are to be content with what our Lord gives us. We can be confident that He will provide what we need.

Right at the climax of this call to continue in the life of faith and to not be drawn back into Judaism is one of the greatest promises given to us in the Bible: "Never will I leave you" (Hebrews 13:5). To make sure the reader doesn't miss the importance of this statement, the author uses a Greek construction that could not be more emphatic. With a redundant pronoun he writes, "He Himself says." The verb used is an imperfect. In the Greek, the imperfect tense shows linear and continuous action. So a literal translation could be, "He says, that is Himself speaking now, and He continues to say forever: never will I leave you."

We don't have to compete for acceptance, and we don't have to worry when we falter, because we are never alone. The author goes on to encourage us by echoing the confession of the psalmist, "The LORD is with me; I will not be afraid" (see Psalm 118:6–7). We can relax. But the good news doesn't stop there. This verse finishes with the question "What can man do to me?" Essentially, the author of Hebrews is saying, "You can't do anything of consequence to me, because my Lord is here to protect me."

1. Jewish Christians were facing persecution at this time from both Jews and Gentiles, tempting them to return to their Jewish communities. Read the promise in light of their social and physical afflictions. Write down the emphatic words found in Hebrews 13:5–6.

2. The author warns us about the dangers of materialism. Some Israelites cherished materialistic hopes as a sign of God's kingdom and saw material wealth as a sign of God's approval. How does materialism threaten our hope?

3. The birth of Christianity was complicated, and house churches struggled to stay connected to other sister churches. Gentiles were being converted. Jews were still practicing their customs but also following Christianity. Relationships were strained, and it was important to know that God was going to be faithful to these early believers, no matter what. How did the exhortation in Ephesians 2:11–13 bring about the unity they needed?

> Therefore, remember that formerly you who are Gentiles by birth and called "uncircumcised" by those who call themselves "the circumcision" (that done in the body by the hands of men)—remember that at that time you were separate from Christ, excluded from citizenship in Israel and foreigners to the covenants of the promise, without hope and without God in the world. But now in Christ Jesus you who once were far away have been brought near through the blood of Christ.
> —Ephesians 2:11–13

⁂ EMBRACING THE PROMISE ⁂

We often forget to ask for help when we need it the most. Take a moment to read these verses that petition for God's quick help.

- But you, O LORD, be not far off; O my Strength, come quickly to help me. (Psalm 22:19)

- Answer me quickly, O LORD; my spirit fails. (Psalm 143:7)

※ **PRAYER** ※

Father, rescue me when my spirit fails and my hope falters. Shelter me when my emotions and fears move to the forefront of my mind. And help me to be a calming presence, a woman who is sure of Your love for me, to the people You've put in my life.

DAY 3

MISPLACED HOPE

God has said, "Never will I leave you; never will I forsake you." So we say with confidence, "The Lord is my helper; I will not be afraid. What can man do to me?"

—Hebrews 13:5–6

※ RECONNECTING WITH THE PROMISE ※

In the 1960s, a new theology was emerging among German theologians, a theology of hope. Scholars were trying to understand the mission of the church. Jürgen Moltmann, who was deeply impacted by Deitrich Bonhoeffer, wrote *A Theology of Hope*, which was a theological perspective with an eschatological or end-times foundation, focusing on the hope that the resurrection brings as well as the future return of Christ.

This theology was also concerned with the condition of the world impacted by sin, so there was a clear acknowledgment of humanity's depraved nature. To move toward hope, believers need to accept the truth that we are broken. If we ignore this fact, we can fall prey to misplacing hope and pursuing temporal victories aside from our true hope found in Jesus Christ.

Hope has to do with our future. There is an acceptance that there will be tension and discord in this world because of our sinful condition, but not to the point of despair. Christ is the author of our hope.

> Eschatology: the doctrine or study of the "last things"; a belief concerning the ultimate or final things, such as death, the destiny of humanity, the Second Coming, or the Last Judgment.

⬛ A Christian should find hope in the future but also experience much discontentment with the way the world is now. Write down some areas of discontentment that we live with. How can this week's promise keep us from pushing too far toward despair?

> Praise be to the God and Father of our Lord Jesus Christ! In his great mercy he has given us new birth into a living hope through the resurrection of Jesus Christ from the dead.
>
> —1 Peter 1:3

⬛ How does hope for the future bring about a hope for today?

⫷ UNDERSTANDING GOD'S PROMISES ⫸

Throughout the Bible God uses time, events, and people to bring about His hope. And sometimes He has to intervene and stop us dead in our tracks when we have misplaced our hope. This happened in Genesis, when God's people thought their hope could be found in the man-made empires and contrived human securities.

Read Genesis 11:1–9.

The tower was likely a ziggurat, a common pyramidlike structure with steps and ramps leading up the sides. It was built as a monument to the people's greatness, so it could be seen easily in a city. This tower was clearly an attempt to bring glory to the builders, not to God. They failed to recognize that without God, they had no hope. Without Him, they had no shelter. And when their language was confused and their worlds thrown into chaos, they were left isolated and hopeless.

Human achievements do not have to be bad or something that robs us of our hope in Christ. But when we use them for our self-identity and as a means of temporal hope, they can become idols. Idolatry can even seep into our churches. God warned us, "No other gods before Me," because He knew what would destroy us and our hope.

1. The people said, "Come, let us build *ourselves* a city . . . so that we may make a name for ourselves." What misplaced hope can we see in the plan of the people?

2. What monuments, figuratively or literally speaking, do we hold high in our secular culture?

3. Can you identify towers of misplaced hope you have built?

4. From your observations and in light of the scriptures studied today, what misplaced hopes can be found even in the Christian culture of today?

> Christ Himself is the author of all hope: "Paul, an apostle of Christ Jesus by the command of God our Savior and of Christ Jesus our hope, to Timothy my true son in the faith: Grace, mercy and peace from God the Father and Christ Jesus our Lord.
> —1 Timothy 1:1–2

≫ EMBRACING THE PROMISE ≪

Now that you've considered the towers you've built in your own life, consider ways you can begin to tear down those monuments before they confuse your life and block your view of God's glory. Write down three steps you'll take this week.

❧ PRAYER ❧

Pray this verse over you and over someone God has laid on your heart during this study: "May the God of hope fill you with all joy and peace as you trust in him, so that you will overflow with hope by the power of the Holy Spirit" (Romans 15:13).

DAY 4

HOPE FOR ALL GENERATIONS

God has said, "Never will I leave you; never will I forsake
you." So we say with confidence, "The Lord is my helper;
I will not be afraid. What can man do to me?"

—**Hebrews 13:5–6**

❧ RECONNECTING WITH THE PROMISE ❧

As broken people, we struggle to remember the hope we have, or as we discussed yesterday, we tend to misplace our hope. The promise is there for us every day, no matter what season of life we are in. However, it is one thing to try to maintain a sound theology of hope for ourselves, but when we think of our families—children, parents, grandparents—who also are in need of hope, we can become very discouraged. I want us to read this promise of hope for our families and what God wants to do for future generations.

▨ Most families have been affected by the misplaced hope of past generations. Have you ever stopped to think about how your grandparents' relationship with God affects you directly? Or maybe you have and you understand well the generational sin that continues to be passed down in your family. What poor choices continue to impact you or your siblings?

◙ Think about your maternal and paternal ancestors. What relative has had the most powerful influence on your life and why?

◙ We inherit both good and bad legacies from our families. What are some good things you have learned from family members?

⇛ UNDERSTANDING GOD'S PROMISES ⇚

The term *generational sin* comes from the "law of generations," which God revealed to Moses and is interestingly present in nearly every religious system. That the law of generations is true seems to receive worldwide recognition. How it works is another matter, but for our purposes today, we want to look at patterns, attitudes, actions, beliefs, and habits that we have inherited or observe being passed down to the next generation in our families.

The good news is we don't have to pass down sinful learned behavior, whether it is patterns of addiction, abuse, or negativity. It can stop with us. But before we can do that, we have to recognize the misplaced hopes in our family members around us. However, let me clarify. Let's say your maternal grandmother was an alcoholic. Your mother is not responsible for that sin until she partakes in passing down that cycle. So often when we don't understand how to deal with generational sin or behaviors, the cycle continues.

Read Exodus 34:5–7.

1. It would be easy to believe that our family is doomed and that God is angry with us, but that is not our Father's heart. How does this passage dispel the notion that God in the Old Testament is merely vengeful?

2. Sin is one of the biggest reasons our hope for life turns to despair. As discussed, some sins are just passed down, but not as punishment from God. Sins such as greed, anger, and selfishness also can be patterns of living that we learn. Can you identify patterns or behaviors that you are determined not to repeat in your own immediate family?

Read Nehemiah 1:4–11.

Nehemiah received word that Jerusalem was again in shambles, both physically and spiritually. This burdened his heart profoundly, and he wept for many days. In verse 6, Nehemiah cried out, "I confess the sin we Israelites, including myself and my father's house, have committed against you" (v. 6). He is then granted permission to return to his homeland on a mission of restoration.

3. All of us at one time or another have felt like our families were in shambles. Are there areas of sin in your family that you believe are unconfessed? Bring your grief to God for the spiritual concerns you have for future generations.

4. Old patterns of behavior that you have seen in your family of origin may not affect you or you children right now, but when we don't acknowledge them before God, they have a way of appearing at unexpected times. Have you been surprised to see that you have done something you vowed to never repeat, a habit of your mother or father?

⇒ EMBRACING THE PROMISE ⇐

There is nothing more powerful in restoring our hope than the Word of God. I often pray Scripture over my son, Christian, and there are no better prayers a mother could offer. I've selected a few verses here for you to pray over family members who are on your heart, who are in need of the hope of Jesus.

- Acts 2:25–26: "God, I pray that _____ will see the Lord always before (him/her). Because You are at _____'s right hand, (he/she) will not be shaken. Therefore _____'s heart is glad and (his/her) tongue rejoices; (his/her) body also will live in hope."

- Titus 1:2: "I pray that _____ would have a faith and knowledge resting on the hope of eternal life, which God, who does not lie, promised before the beginning of time."

- 2 Thessalonians 2:16–17: "Lord, may Jesus Christ himself and God our Father, who loved us and by his grace gave us eternal encouragement and good hope, encourage _____'s heart and strengthen (him/her) in every good deed and word."

> I, the LORD your God, am a jealous God, punishing the children for the sin of the fathers to the third and fourth generation of those who hate me, but showing love to a thousand generations of those who love me and keep my commandments.
> —Deuteronomy 5:9–10

⇒ PRAYER ⇐

Heavenly Father, continue to reveal to me the patterns of sin that permeate my life. Give me the strength and discernment to rid myself of them, and instead cling to Your love and hope. In Your precious Son's name, amen.

DAY 5

HOPE OF COMMUNITY

God has said, "Never will I leave you; never will I forsake you."
So we say with confidence, "The Lord is my helper; I will not be
afraid. What can man do to me? What can man do to me?"

—Hebrews 13:5–6

⫷ RECONNECTING WITH THE PROMISE ⫸

In our discussion on cultivating a theology of hope in our lives, we mentioned the Greek word *elpis*, which means hope. In Greek mythology, Elpis was the personification of hope, but she was seen as an extension of suffering—not a good thing. And when we think of the modern use of the word in our culture, it is a temporal state: "I hope to get there on time," or "I am holding out hope that we can turn this sinking ship around." But in the New Testament, *elpis* is used to mean a collective hope in the body of Christ. The Thessalonians are exhorted to hope for reunion with their deceased brethren (1 Thessalonians 4:13–18) and to minister hope to one another (2 Corinthians 1:7).

It is a mystery how we bring each other toward the hope of God. As I have the overwhelming joy of sharing my heart and life with other women, their stories and testimonies bring about new hope in my heart and hope for others. Have you noticed in Scripture how Jesus will often tell individuals to go and tell their testimonies to others? He knew our shared experiences would edify us toward living in community and pressing on toward our eternal hope. The Christ in you that you allow me to see changes me and edifies the body of believers.

Romans 8:16–17 says, "The Spirit himself testifies with our spirit that we are God's children. Now if we are children, then we are heirs—heirs of God and co-heirs with Christ, if indeed we share in his sufferings in order that we may also share in his glory."

Most of us know how we may have to force ourselves to crawl into the doors of our church on Sunday morning because we often are so tired. But then a mysterious thing happens. It really doesn't matter if the pastor hit a home-run sermon or the choir sounded spectacular. We are nourished because we have gathered in His name. He renews our hearts with His hope.

▨ Think about the last worship service you attended. In what ways was God faithful to encourage you? Was it a word in season from a friend? Was it the opportunity to participate in worship with other believers?

⫸ UNDERSTANDING GOD'S PROMISES ⫷

Christians are to be seen as the people of hope; even nonbelievers expect us to have hope. We have hope in the God who is present and in His promises. We gather together because of our hope in Christ. The earliest eyewitnesses of the resurrected Jesus couldn't help but share their hope.

In day 1, we looked at hope through the eyes of Mary Magdalene. Jesus first appeared to her in the garden, and she didn't recognize Him at first, as the Scripture says, because of her own pain (John 20:14). But as soon as she realized who He was, she went and told others about her resurrected hope. And then Jesus began appearing to others. One by one, the good news was being told, and through the community of believers, hope was set ablaze in the hearts of humanity for all eternity.

Read Luke 24:13–49.

1. In light of this passage, how does God use community to reveal His hope to us?

2. The two followers in this passage missed the significance and greatest display of hope in the history of humanity because they were so focused on their disappointment and problems. Can you think of a time when this has been true for you?

So we hold on to this promise that God has given us: that He will never leave us, never forsake us. Christ embraced all the deathly leaving and forsaking for us so that we never need be alone.

—Sheila Walsh, *The Shelter of God's Promises* DVD

During this week, we have seen our inherent need to look to Jesus as our one and only hope. How easy it is to misplace our hope in things that promise us temporal relief. I pray that this has been a week when you have had a chance to build your own theology of hope and reinforce this promise with a fresh look at His Word. There is hope for you, for your family, for those who are far away from the Lord.

⟫ EMBRACING THE PROMISE ⟪

Despite the rapid spread of Christianity and its continuous witness over the past two thousand years, people still refuse to believe in Jesus Christ. For many, it takes the hope of another to push someone toward the hope of Christ. Think about the person you prayed for during our lesson on grace. Review your notes and the scriptures you highlighted. What hope can you share with this person in more specific ways?

⟫ PRAYER ⟪

Lord, thank You that You bring people into our lives to reinforce the hope of You when we cannot see it. Thank You for the power of our testimony and how the real lives of others fuel hope in us. Use me, Lord, to be a voice of hope to my family and to those around me. In Your mighty name, amen.

THE PROMISE OF STRENGTH

I FEEL THINGS ARE CRASHING AROUND ME

> In this world you will have trouble. But take
> heart! I have overcome the world.
>
> —John 16:33

DAY 1

THE PROMISE OF STRENGTH

In this world you will have trouble. But take
heart! I have overcome the world.

—John 16:33

What may seem to be discouraging to us, Jesus offers as encouragement. There is nothing that can happen to you today or tomorrow that hasn't passed through the merciful hands of God. Even when we suffer for a time, we will always be victorious because of the battle Christ has won. So take heart and have courage; we are strong women of God because He gives us His strength.

VIDEO
25 MINUTES

Watch session 8 on the Shelter of God's Promises *DVD. Keep your Bible nearby for reference and take notes in this book as needed. Fill in the blanks below as you listen to Sheila's message.*

- In this world you will have *trouble*. But take heart! I have *overcome* the world. (John 16:33)

- God's plan, from the very beginning, was to *overcome* the world—not with *force* but with *Love* —a violent *Love* stronger than death; one that waters cannot quench or rivers overflow.

- All the way from *Genesis* to *Revelation*, since it has been our inability to *cover* ourselves, Christ *covers* us by the washing of his blood.

- God is *very present* in the moments of *deepest grief*, and His arms are wide and clasping—they are strong enough to *keep* us, and strong enough to *lift* us from this world.

*John 13:1
Having Loved his own he Loved
them to the end.*

148

KEY CONCEPTS

The circumstances surrounding our promise verse in John 16:

"For as the sufferings of Christ abound in us, so our consolation also abounds through Christ" (2 Corinthians 1:5 NKJV):

"I do not ask that you take them out of the world, but that you keep them from the evil one" (John 17:15):

MY NOTES

SMALL GROUP DISCUSSION
25 MINUTES

Break into small groups and discuss the following questions:

1. In John 16, the disciples didn't realize that Jesus' death was very near and His earthly life was going to come crashing down around them. Even though He warned them, "You will have trouble," they were most likely blindsided in the days that followed. Can you identify a moment in your life when you were blindsided by trouble and just didn't see it coming?

2. In His words to the disciples in John 16, Jesus was trying to prepare His friends for what was about to happen and emphasize to them: "Take heart!" (v. 33). For you personally, what does it mean today for you to "take heart"?

3. Amy Carmichael said, "God leads us by unexpected ways, off the strong, solid land."[1] When we are facing trouble, sometimes the Lord maneuvers us through routes we thought we could never survive. Can you recall such a time in your life?

Bonus Question: Jesus was telling His disciples to lean into Him for strength. What would cause us to resist such a loving invitation?

LOOKING DEEPER
10 MINUTES

Dig deeper into Scripture to understand the context of this promise.

These are strange comments if they're meant to impart peace:

- "You will have trouble" (see John 16:33).

- "I will leave you" (see John 16:7).

- "Men will want to kill you" (see John 16:2).

They're not the kinds of sentiments you see on greeting cards or T-shirts. But it's the message Christ gave His disciples in their final days together. He wanted them to know what they were going to face, because, as the 1980s *G. I. Joe* cartoon reminded us, "Knowing is half the battle." This divine knowledge—which was summed up in the three years' worth of Jesus' teaching—would be the basis of strength for the disciples. They'd been taught well what kingdom living was like, and the time was coming to put that knowledge into practice.

But the knowledge alone wouldn't be enough. They needed a Comforter, a Guide to mentor them through their darkest hours. The Holy Spirit came down to dwell among us; He is the One we find our strength in when we think we have none left.

PERSONAL REFLECTION
5 MINUTES

Meditate on the following questions and hear what God is teaching you through His Word and through your study group. Share your insights with the group, if you feel comfortable doing so.

In John 16, Jesus teaches the disciples about the Holy Spirit. Read verses 12–14. In what ways has the Holy Spirit revealed God's glory to you? Have you ever heard a message from the Holy Spirit?

LIVING THE PROMISE
5 MINUTES

Discuss ways to apply what you've learned this week with your group.

Jesus says, "I have overcome the world" (John 16:33); therefore, we are overcomers as well. There may be some in your group or your community who need God's strength in this hour and the battle is beginning. Take time to pray for one another this week.

PRAYER
5 MINUTES

Take time to pray with your group to close the session.

God, give us the strength to overcome the trials we face day in and day out. You've promised us peace, love, grace, and hope, and we believe You'll give us the strength we need as well. Thank You for Your merciful gifts, Father. May we use them to Your glory.

DAY 2

THE STRENGTH FOUND IN SUFFERING

In this world you will have trouble. But take
heart! I have overcome the world.

—John 16:33

≫ RECONNECTING WITH THE PROMISE ≪

Life's greatest trials often come without a moment's notice. There is no prep time or
convenient moment to book them on our daily calendars. They brutishly make their
way into our lives and threaten to undo us. But suffering is often the very thing that
allows our lives to be resurrected. When we look back, those moments can become
milestones and strong pillars of our testimony because we survived by His strength
alone.

Today we will look at the ways in which Jesus was preparing His disciples for His
departure, even though there was no way they could fully realize what was to come.

Look back at the chart on page 74 and write out a praise to God here for each of
the items you listed in the chart.

≫ UNDERSTANDING GOD'S PROMISES ≪

John gives us such a compelling image of Jesus and His ministry. He takes the infi-
nite and pushes it into the temporal scope of the story. He recounts the ministry of
Jesus in a personal way but doesn't limit the text to just those years. John keeps the
past in view, such as the history of the Israelites and the prophets. He even takes us
to prehistoric times: "In the beginning was the Word" (John 1:1). The gospel of John

152

is multilayered in the understanding of time and meaning. The author gives us an earthly account and a spiritual account of Jesus' teachings.

Read John 16:16–33.

"But these are written that you may believe that Jesus is the Christ, the Son of God, and that by believing you may have life in his name" (John 20:31). This verse shows us the purpose of John's gospel, to show us the need for spiritual birth, which gives us an eternal heritage with God.

John 16 is Jesus' last discourse with the Twelve, and our promise for this week is the final statement Jesus makes to the disciples together. He has just revealed that He will be taken from them, and in the previous verse He prophesied their dispersion. At the same time, He has told them that they will abandon Him but His Father will not leave Him. He is teaching them about the amazing gift of the Holy Spirit.

What may seem to be discouraging to us, Jesus offers as encouragement. He tells them they are to be left behind and then scattered, but by predicting this hard time, He gives them hope for later, when it will come as less of a shock to them. Their Teacher can see into the future, and even though He must suffer, He will have victory. The world may bring tribulation on them, but Jesus has conquered the world. You see, the tribulation that the world will bring is really just the beginning of the final victory of the returning conqueror, Jesus. He is their model. He will endure His suffering patiently, waiting for the time of the final confrontation, obedient to the will of the Father, and continuing in His sacrificial love for His followers. They are to take heart, knowing that He will overcome in the end.

KEY PLAYERS OF THE PROMISE

John—The author of this book was the one referred to as Jesus' beloved disciple. Six of the miracles recorded in John are unique to the other Gospels. He knew amazing details about Jesus and His life, and he knew Jerusalem in great detail. Scholars have attempted to harmonize Matthew, Mark, and Luke with John, but because John wrote this gospel to be more than a book about events and a narrative, it cannot be treated quite like the others.

Jesus—In the gospel of John, the author emphasizes Jesus was fully man and fully God. The Christology of Jesus is central to the book, making Jesus the focus.

1. In John 16:29–33, Jesus is talking directly to His disciples. We often get the impression they were confused by Jesus' sayings and teachings. But they told Jesus they believed that He came from God, a first step toward a great power in their lives. How did your first steps of faith strengthen you?

2. We know, as disciples, that we will feel out of sync with the world, and some of our earthly suffering with come from this reality. Today, what hardships in your life have resulted from simply being a disciple?

After Jesus' suffering on the cross and the resurrection, the disciples' understanding of their faith was much deeper and the Holy Spirit was now their personal Counselor. We see how the Spirit emboldened the disciples as they spoke with greater authority after Jesus' ascension. The resurrection made all the difference. The disciples' strength came from Jesus' conquering of sin and death.

3. The resurrection power of Jesus allows us to experience His strength. Think about the corners of your heart that have been depleted of strength, that perhaps have grown cold and need the resurrection power of Jesus. Write them down here.

⇛ EMBRACING THE PROMISE ⇚

You lift weights at the gym to gain physical strength, so let's get in the habit of lifting spiritual weights to strengthen ourselves in our hearts and minds. Memorize a passage of Scripture (this week's verse, John 16:33, is a great place to start). Read a commentary on a passage you're studying. Even doing this study is working those faith muscles!

⇛ PRAYER ⇚

Lord, thank You for the power we can find in Your suffering and resurrection. Lead my heart toward a greater revelation of Your strength. Help me to grasp the truth that no trial has the power to consume me. Your strength is enough for today. In Jesus' name, amen.

> Do you not know?
>   Have you not heard?
> The LORD is the everlasting God,
>   the Creator of the ends of the earth.
> He will not grow tired or weary,
>   and his understanding no one can fathom.
> He gives strength to the weary
>   and increases the power of the weak.
> Even youths grow tired and weary,
>   and young men stumble and fall;
> but those who hope in the LORD
>   will renew their strength.
> They will soar on wings like eagles;
>   they will run and not grow weary,
>   they will walk and not be faint.
>
> —Isaiah 40:28–31

DAY 3

THE STRENGTH IN SUBMISSION

In this world you will have trouble. But take
heart! I have overcome the world.

—John 16:33

⇶ RECONNECTING WITH THE PROMISE ⇶

I believe the strength of each of our lives comes down to a handful of life-changing moments.

Laurie's Story

For Laurie's family, the biggest life-changing moment to date came one hour after their twenty-week ultrasound when, in the midst of announcing to family and friends the news she would be having a girl, her doctor called to tell her that her precious baby's brain was measuring abnormally.

Through disbelief and tears, she and her husband prepared for their visit to the specialist the next day. She was adamant that before she found out any additional news about her baby's condition, she needed to be named—her daughter became Julia Anne.

Julia's condition was difficult for the doctors to pinpoint, and the remainder of the pregnancy was spent visiting specialists to measure her brain and make best guesses. Looking back now, Laurie remembers being happy during this time despite the unknown; she believes they were numbed with grace, covered with a calm that could not come from themselves, and granted strength beyond their own ability. She had fears but she also felt hopeful about Julia Anne's life and purpose.

As the due date approached, news around Julia's condition became a bit more serious. She wasn't growing and the ultrasound was finding more abnormalities in her brain. Laurie could sense her doctor getting increasingly nervous, so a date was set to induce. Three days prior to induction she went in for a routine appointment and was seen by a doctor who had not been following their case. In his attempt to be helpful, he cautioned Laurie that Julia might not be "salvageable." He suggested she be prepared to make end-of-life decisions at her birth. This was, of course, the one

THE STRENGTH IN SUBMISSION

appointment she went to alone, and the doctor's words rocked her to her core. She was devastated by his warning and his sterile terminology. She wondered if she had been naive to be so hopeful about Julia's chances.

Julia was born, or more accurately, yanked out with forceps, on June 22, 2007, around 2:00 in the afternoon. A room full of nurses and doctors awaited her arrival, all fully prepared for her to be instantly swept away to the NICU for intervention. Instead, this little five-pound five-ounce lady came out looking super pink and super healthy. One by one, the unneeded nurses left the room and Laurie and her husband, Wes, were left to stare in awe and wonder at their new favorite person. In that moment they knew God's strength was cradled around Julia—and them.

When Julia was eight weeks old, the results of a blood test done at birth came back and they received an official diagnosis of a rare chromosome disorder. Once again their lives were turned upside down by just a phone call. Julia's condition was not something she would grow out of or something that would just disappear. Their little girl was formed with a different set of blueprints than most of us—the doctors did not have other cases of her disorder to tell them about. None existed. So they would have to let Julia tell them how her journey would unfold.

> Often part of our struggle is letting the unknown pieces unfold and order our lives around an unforeseen set of blueprints. What strength comes to us when we let go of our ideal?

≫ UNDERSTANDING GOD'S PROMISES ≪

This promise is a reminder to us that our testing and struggles will be a part of this life until Jesus returns to us and that there is indeed strength to carry us as we submit to God.

Read Matthew 26:36–46.

In this passage, darkness is looming over Jesus. Confusion, sorrow, and overwhelming agony are expressed in Jesus' honest prayers to His Father. Jesus was seeking comfort from His community. But instead He suffered at the hands of a close associate and disciple, Judas. But this can improve our perspective and encourage us when we experience rejection and betrayal from those we think we can count on.

1. What does the text say the disciples were doing? What was Jesus' response?

fell asleep

2. Jesus asked His Father to remove the cup of suffering, to find another way to save the world. This doesn't reveal a rebellion against God but rather the terrible suffering He was enduring while clothed in humanity. How does this passage depict a perfect example of the strength in submission, complete surrender to God's will?

> Jesus' agony was worse than death because He paid for all sin by being separated from His Father.

He had already choosen his path.

3. What does it take for you to get to the place where you say, "I want Your will to be done, God, not mine"? How did Jesus get to that place?

Laurie's Story, continued

The second layer of the diagnosis Julia Anne received involved finding out that her disorder came directly from Laurie, her mother; she was the carrier of the gene that caused Julia's condition. Pile on the layers of grief! Self-loathing and guilt came gushing in—they had a source to blame, and it was Laurie. She remembers lying in bed wanting to scratch all of her skin off, knowing every cell of her body carried this hardship for her little daughter. *What is my husband really thinking? Does he hate me? Will he reject me? What does this mean for our future, for the rest of our children?* All these thoughts on top of her biggest fear: *What does this mean for Julia?*

The fear, the grief, the shame all had the potential to destroy Laurie. The provision of strength from God preserved her.

Many people who loved them during this time reassured them of God's promise to heal. Their prayers were for a miracle in which Julia would be changed. Laurie cringed at these promises. Not because she didn't believe God could do what they said; she just didn't feel that was the miracle they needed. At that time she needed God to do more than remove her pain; she needed to feel God in the midst of pain. Wasn't that what was in the Bible? *In this life there will be trouble, there will be pain?* The miracle she needed was to feel His strength within her pain, to be sustained in the midst of it. She felt that the miracle would come in the form of His strength.

Just as He provided manna to the Israelites, God daily is providing Laurie with the strength she needs to face trials and pain. When she has tried to hoard this strength to carry into the next day, it quickly crumbles. Questions like "What if her seizures come back?" "Will I be able to do this when she is ten?" "What will I do if she dies?"—all these lead her into fear and doubt and destroy the strength she's been given. So Laurie trusts that God will provide strength for each day.

Laurie realized that Julia did not need to be changed by a miracle; she did. She needed to be taught, and God sent her a teacher in the form of a five-pound baby girl with a special brain, special eyes, special ways of moving, and special ways of communicating to teach her that she is not on her own, and that each of us is capable of far more than we imagine when He is our strength.

> He has come to bring revolution, and . . . it must begin in our hearts. It must start not by mustering more of [our] own strength for the battle but by relying upon His.
>
> —Sheila Walsh, *The Shelter of God's Promises* DVD

4. With God's strength, we are capable of overcoming the impossible. Suffering accentuates God's strength. How does Laurie's story point you to the strength of Jesus and the power of surrender?

5. What teachers has God brought your way to illuminate the strength of God?

⇛ EMBRACING THE PROMISE ⇚

Where in your life are you relying on your own strength? What will you do today to rely more on God's strength as you struggle with the trials of life?

⇛ PRAYER ⇚

Lord, the hardest prayer to pray is "Your will be done." Give me strength to pray this daily. I have been bought with a high price and this is no longer my life to live, but Yours. May my life be a testimony of Your strength. In Your powerful name, amen.

DAY 4

HIS FIRM GRIP

In this world you will have trouble. But take
heart! I have overcome the world.

—John 16:33

⇛ RECONNECTING WITH THE PROMISE ⇚

It is one thing to say, "The Lord is my shepherd, I shall not be in want" (Psalm 23:1). It is quite another to find yourself in a dark place and discover that you are not alone—when you truly begin to rely on God's promise tucked into Psalm 23:3–4: "Even though I walk through the valley of the shadow of death, I will fear no evil, for you are with me; your rod and your staff, they comfort me."

My walk through the valley of the shadow of death began like this. In one day I went from being the cohost of a nationally syndicated talk show to being in a psychiatric ward of a hospital by that evening. Earlier this week we learned that we don't always get much notice before crisis hits.

Climbing back out of a hole that deep is hard, and there are many painful truths to face as you make the climb. A pivotal time in my life revolved around dealing with depression. If you haven't suffered from serious depression, I think it's hard to understand the physical and mental pain involved. Much of depression is silent and isolating and . . . within. A brain tumor shows up on a CT scan, but depleted brain chemicals do not. Depression is only one of myriad isolating realities.

I think of the woman who has just been told that she cannot have children—the nursery door slams in her face and she will remain an outsider. To the one whose husband looks in her eyes after twenty years of marriage and tells her, "I don't love you anymore. I'm not sure I ever did." Or the woman who looks at herself for the first time in a mirror after the landscape of her femininity has been ravaged by breast cancer. The temptation for those who are looking on is to say, "Pull yourself together. You have so much to be thankful for!" But to those who are in the eye of the storm, that is like saying to a child with a crushed leg, "Get up and walk." As we walk through our troubles, we are promised that His grip is strong and He won't let go of us.

Have there been moments in your life when you felt as if you had let go of God? How did He let you know that He had not let go of you?

⁘ UNDERSTANDING GOD'S PROMISES ⁘

Read Psalm 23.

Psalm 23 is the most well-known and loved of the psalms, so as you read it over, try to read it with a fresh perspective. You may want to try reading it in a version of the Bible that is less familiar to you, so you can better hear the promises of strength that are there.

From the first four verses we know this psalm was written in a place of crisis, possibly when David was fleeing from his son Absalom. Though David's troubles are looming, he writes a poem of thanks to God, who is his protector and strength. The Shepherd imparts new life and strength by His presence alone. The hill country of Judah was broken up by ravines and perilous terrain, which were difficult to traverse. David is saying that God is ever protecting, ever leading, and He knows the best route to take.

1. David first declares, "The LORD is my shepherd" (Psalm 23:1). What images of strength come to mind? In verses 1–4, where are some of the places God leads us? How does this compare to John 16:33?

161

2. In verse 2, he says, "He makes me lie down." Why do you think David could "lie down" in the midst of trouble?

3. God's promise to walk with us "through the valley of the shadow of death" (v. 4) shows us His grip on our lives. His loving protection has a strong hold over us. Why do you think David chose to mention the frightening shadow of death?

4. Jesus refers to Himself as the Good Shepherd (John 10:11). Why is it significant that Jesus is the one to come alongside us when we pass through the valley of the shadow of death?

The shepherd had to take his sheep through the valleys for food and water though it was very dangerous. Wolves, coyotes, and steep terrain put the sheep in harm's way, but the shepherd knows that it is essential for the sheep to keep moving. Sheep are like moving lawn mowers—but they have to go where the grass is to stay alive.

5. God keeps us in a mode of growth and nourishment and takes us to places we could never go on our own. What places of growth, though they may have tried to discourage, has He led you to for nourishment?

⋙ EMBRACING THE PROMISE ⋘

The shepherd's staff, a tall walking stick, was used to snare an animal around the neck, protect the sheep, and keep the sheep within reach of the shepherd's grip. It could even guide a sheep quickly out of a fast-running brook to dry land. The rod was a short stick of leather. It wasn't used to hit or punish, but it was a rod of comfort—keeping mosquitoes and flies away.

What "staffs" and "rods" has God used in your life? How does recognizing them as such impact your daily living?

⋙ PRAYER ⋘

Lord, thank You for your arm of protection. Your arm is long, and it reaches down to me. Thank You that You never let me go, though I often try to leave You. Lead me, Lord, through the steps of this day, and take me to where I need to go. In Jesus' name, amen.

DAY 5

THE JOY OF THE LORD IS MY STRENGTH

In this world you will have trouble. But take
heart! I have overcome the world.

—John 16:33

⋙ RECONNECTING WITH THE PROMISE ⋘

How often do we really stop to think about the joy of the Lord, that His joy can actually be our strength? Joy is a delight given to us by God that runs deeper than pain or pleasure. From a biblical perspective, joy is not tied to external things or circumstances. Both in the Old Testament and in the New Testament, joy is something that marks the life of a follower of God. It is a quality of life, not a fleeting emotion but grounding in God Himself. The joy of God is an expression of one's whole relationship with God, an overwhelming awareness of His presence. It is something too big to keep to ourselves.

There are many things throughout the day that threaten to steal our joy. While God never takes joy away from us, it can be so hidden in our hearts, pushed down, that we forget there is a source of strength that the Holy Spirit deposited in us.

▣ Name some joy robbers in your life that cause you to lose sight of this joy.

⫸ UNDERSTANDING GOD'S PROMISES ⫷

Read Nehemiah 8:5–10.

The exiles began their return from Babylon to Jerusalem in 538 BC. Nehemiah was governor of Judah around 445–433 BC. He followed Ezra, whose mission is dated 458 BC. They were both concerned with what was happening in worship and with the lack of progress in building the walls, which protected a city and provided safety. Ezra arrived with a further group of Jewish returnees to initiate reforms, one of which was the banishment of foreign wives and their children because they were perceived as contaminating the Israelite worship. Meanwhile, back in Susa (Babylon), Nehemiah hears that the walls have not yet been rebuilt and seeks permission to go to Jerusalem to get this work done. He arrives twelve years after Ezra. Nehemiah faces strong opposition to his program of rebuilding and has to cope with other economic and social difficulties, even threats against his life. In spite of this, the building is completed in record time and celebrated with the reading of the Law by Ezra and a celebration of the Feast of Booths.

Nehemiah 8 plays a pivotal role in the book in that the reading of the Law completes the building for Jerusalem and reminds the people of the need for worship and faithfulness to Yahweh. Through the relentless opposition they faced, Nehemiah reminded them that the joy of the Lord was their strength (Nehemiah 8:10).

1. As one of the greatest leaders in the Bible, Nehemiah knew the need to celebrate the victories of God as a community. From this Bible passage, what are some ways he set the atmosphere for God-centered worship?

2. If you read the entire book of Nehemiah, you can read further about all the opposition Nehemiah encountered—enemies, evil rulers, and financial hardship. Through every phase of his calling to the Israelites, he was worshipping God, not just on the days set aside for corporate worship. He was spiritually ready because he didn't withhold praise to God in the midst of trials. How does our daily worship affect our joy?

3. Read Nehemiah 8:9–10. What did the people do when they heard God's Law and realized how far they had moved away from Him?

4. What did Nehemiah tell them to be filled with?

≫ EMBRACING THE PROMISE ≪

When we celebrate and give to others, even when we don't feel like it, we are strengthened spiritually and God's joy rises in us. What joyful offering can you give to God today? Celebrate how He faithfully draws you back to Him, time and time again.

> Joy is a quality of life, not a fleeting emotion. It is grounded in God Himself.

≫ PRAYER ≪

God, give me strength to worship You in all situations in my life. I desire Your joy to be a defining characteristic of myself, and I know that joy comes from the strength of knowing and trusting You. In Jesus' name, amen.

THE PROMISE OF MORE

I KNOW THERE'S SOMETHING BETTER

> Ask and it will be given to you; seek and you will find; knock and the door will be opened to you. For everyone who asks receives; he who seeks finds; and to him who knocks, the door will be opened.
>
> —Matthew 7:7–8

DAY 1

THE PROMISE OF MORE

Ask and it will be given to you; seek and you will find; knock and the door will be opened to you. For everyone who asks receives; he who seeks finds; and to him who knocks, the door will be opened.

—**Matthew 7:7–8**

How many of us have asked God to give us our heart's desire—a husband, security, the health of a child, and so on—only to have God tell us no? The finality of that is shocking and devastating. So what did Jesus mean when he promised that if we ask, it will be given to us (Matthew 7:7)? How are we to make sense of this promise when we've so often seen the opposite occur in our lives?

VIDEO
25 MINUTES

Watch session 9 on the Shelter of God's Promises *DVD. Keep your Bible nearby for reference and take notes in this book as needed. Fill in the blanks below as you listen to Sheila's message.*

- ▣ _ask_ and it will be given to you; _given_ and you will find; _____ and the door will be opened to you. For everyone who asks _recieves_ ; he who seeks _finds_ ; and to him who knocks, the _door_ will be opened. (Matthew 7:7–8)

- ▣ For "seek," He used the word _Ze teo_, meaning to seek after, look for, strive to find. _applied action_

- ▣ For "knock," He used the word _Krouo_, meaning to knock at the door with a heavy blow.

- ▣ For "ask," Jesus used the word aiteo, meaning "to _entreat_, to beg, or to supplicate."

168

◼ Jesus was saying: __*run*__ to God. *Chase* Him down. Bang on His door anytime, day or night.

KEY CONCEPTS

blessed: *deune joy and pure happiness inner security inner rest*

Pharisaic teaching: *624 laws to obide by*

lex talionis:

hypocrite:

> And that is when Jesus does the most remarkable thing yet. He looks at the crowd, and I can only imagine the love contained in His eyes, and says, "Do not worry about your life."
>
> —Sheila Walsh, *The Shelter of God's Promises* DVD

MY NOTES

SMALL GROUP DISCUSSION
25 MINUTES

Break into small groups and discuss the following questions:

1. Is it difficult for you to "ask" God and honestly believe He hears you? Why or why not?

2. Can you identify moments in your life when you have asked God for something important and He seemed not to answer? What does that make you feel about God? How does that make you feel about your own life and value to God?

3. Think about the things you have asked God to give you recently. What do you think they will help you accomplish in your life?

4. At the end of chapter 7, the text says the crowds were amazed at Jesus' teaching. Do you find Jesus' invitation in Matthew 7:7–9 amazing, or do you find it more confusing?

> Jesus was saying, "Shout to God. Run to Him. Chase Him down. Bang on His door anytime, day or night. Live higher, with all your heart, but lean harder on God, with all that's in you, and you will find God there—always ready, ever waiting to give to you—even beyond what you need." You can't do it by yourself; it's impossible, and that's the whole point. It's not about us, never has been, never will be . . . It's all about God.
>
> —Sheila Walsh, *The Shelter of God's Promises* DVD

LOOKING DEEPER
10 MINUTES

Dig deeper into Scripture to understand the context of this promise.

Read 1 Samuel 8.

The Israelites had just begun to settle down in the promised land, and they were starting to feel at home there. But they, just like most of us, quickly started to compare themselves to their neighbors. But they weren't envious of their homes and cars—they wanted a *king*.

Up until now, they'd been ruled by God alone. Moses and Joshua and the others had been His mouthpiece, but it was clear that even they weren't above the law (as Moses wasn't allowed into the promised land for violating the heart of God's command). But they weren't satisfied being different and following a King they couldn't see. The Israelites wanted a human king they could show off and parade around. God told them no, but they insisted. Finally, He relented and gave them what they wanted.

PERSONAL REFLECTION
5 MINUTES

Meditate on the following questions and hear what God is teaching you through His Word and through your study group. Share your insights with the group, if you feel comfortable doing so.

Has God ever given you something you asked for even if it wasn't what you needed? What happened to make you realize you should have been content with what He offered you instead?

LIVING THE PROMISE
5 MINUTES

Discuss ways to apply what you've learned this week with your group.

Look back over the chart in which you listed your needs in session 2 (page 37). With the Personal Reflection question in mind, are there any items on this list you would change?

PRAYER
5 MINUTES

Take time to pray with your group to close the session.

Pray together, and call out some of God's names in Scripture: I AM, Jehovah Jireh (God who provides), Counselor, Savior, Prince of Peace, El Roi (God who sees). All of these give us a glimpse of why He is able to know what to give to His children. Close your prayer by affirming your trust in Him.

A LASTING KIND OF MORE

Ask and it will be given to you; seek and you will find; knock and
the door will be opened to you. For everyone who asks receives; he
who seeks finds; and to him who knocks, the door will be opened.

—Matthew 7:7–8

⋙ RECONNECTING WITH THE PROMISE ⋘

In this week of study, I encourage you to be as open and honest with God as you can
be. In sesssion 2, we studied the promise of provision and know that He loves it when
His children come to Him, the Source, and simply ask. And with that, we do want
to begin to prayerfully look at our requests and how to listen to Him in the midst of
asking for more.

There may be areas of your life that feel unfulfilled. You may be thinking, *So
what is the point of waiting for God's answer? Have I been pursuing things more than
God? Have I been trying to run ahead of God? What is all my life at this moment leading toward?*

▨ Write out a short reflection paragraph that explains your thoughts on where you
believe God wants to take you and where your life is headed. In light of this,
what does "more" look like for you?

⋙ UNDERSTANDING GOD'S PROMISES ⋘

Read Matthew 7:7–8.

Matthew groups the various teachings of Jesus into five discourses. The Sermon
on the Mount is the foundational teaching that reveals what is expected of those who
are His disciples in the kingdom of heaven. This week's promise is found in the last

chapter of this discourse, and Jesus is telling the people what characteristics they are to develop and how they are to use discretion in their interactions with others. How are they to do it? Return to the Source of all truth.

In this context of needing wisdom and showing behavior worthy of the kingdom, Jesus points to the Father and encourages the people to seek His provision. These two verses are very interesting. In verse 7, there are three imperative verbs, all in the present tense. In verse 8, three particles mirror the verbs in verse 7. We are to pray and pray continually. Three times He tells us to continue in our prayers: "Ask . . . seek . . . knock." Then in verse 8 again we are told to "ask . . . seek . . . knock." The promised results in verse 7 are "it will be given to you . . . you will find . . . it will be opened." And in verse 8 "receives . . . finds . . . the door will by opened."

So Jesus has laid out the objectives of the kingdom and the characteristics of those who are His followers. He then says that to accomplish these goals we must seek what we need from the author of this program—God. And God cannot deny what He has established. We are to persist in seeking those things the Father desires. Our Father, like any parent, will not withhold good things from us.

Jesus is acknowledging the economy of the kingdom in light of these verses. It is not understood by worldly standards. So to truly grasp this teaching, you have to enter the kingdom, which affects your heart, your attitude, what you are living for. He is speaking to the disciples to draw them into His perspective and His truth about life. To understand this promise, you have to be living as a disciple of Jesus.

1. In Matthew 7:7, why do you think God repeats Himself and emphasizes the need to keep asking, to keep pursuing Him?

2. The word for "seek" in this passage can be translated "to run after." What does running after God mean to you?

3. In this passage, Jesus assures us we are rewarded for seeking Him. Which disciples needed to truly seek God with all of their hearts?

4. Read Matthew 7:1–6, the verse preceding the promise. What conditions are there for realizing this promise in our lives?

⁂ EMBRACING THE PROMISE ⁂

As we move deeper into our study, we will look more at the ways God answers prayers in the depths of our lives, not in the shallows. His "more" is always the kind that has lasting impact on us.

How has God answered a prayer for you this week?

⁂ PRAYER ⁂

Write down a short prayer regarding what you are asking for, whether it is an open door for a new opportunity, daily provision, or a miracle. We will revisit this request on day 5 to see if this focused time of seeking has brought part of the answer or if your request has changed.

DAY 3

TOO EASY TO PLEASE

Ask and it will be given to you; seek and you will find; knock and the door will be opened to you. For everyone who asks receives; he who seeks finds; and to him who knocks, the door will be opened.

—Matthew 7:7–8

⁂ RECONNECTING WITH THE PROMISE ⁂

I don't claim to know all there is to know about how God works out each promise in our lives. At times we have to make peace with the fact that we will be confused by God's ways. Sometimes we may find ourselves arguing our case to God, convinced that what we are asking for is exactly what we need. Yet even when God does not answer as we wish, He does use the act of seeking, the process of asking, to change us.

Do you feel like you are pounding on the door and He just seems to be giving you a deaf ear, while you keep standing there with bleeding knuckles? I want to suggest one reason that I believe He may *not* be opening that door you are knocking on. Sometimes our vision for our life, our appetite for more, is too weak for Him. We aren't hungry enough. You may have heard your mom say, "No snacks this close to dinner. You need to be good and hungry so you will eat everything." God doesn't just want to pacify our whims; He has a bigger idea for our life. I love how C. S. Lewis puts it in *The Weight of Glory*:

> If there lurks in most modern minds the notion that to desire our own good and earnestly to hope for the enjoyment of it is a bad thing, I submit that this notion has crept in from Kant and the Stoics and is no part of the Christian faith. Indeed, if we consider the unblushing promises of reward and the staggering nature of the rewards promised in the Gospels, it would seem that our Lord finds our desires, not too strong, but too weak. We are half-hearted creatures, fooling about with drink and sex and ambition when infinite joy is offered us, like an ignorant child who wants to go on making mud pies in a slum because he cannot imagine what is meant by the offer of a holiday at the sea. We are far too easily pleased.[1]

Read over the prayer you wrote yesterday. After reading this quote, do you feel like you may be "too easily pleased" in what you are asking God for?

⫸ UNDERSTANDING GOD'S PROMISES ⫷

We can really miss God and not realize it because our focus is inward, toward ourselves. I think one of the greatest tragedies we read about is that the religious leaders in Jesus' day, most of the Pharisees and Jews, were looking, seeking, and waiting for the Messiah. But they missed God altogether because they were pitching way below heaven, toward their own human desires for someone to come and rescue them from Roman rule. Throughout Jesus' ministry, His identity was a question in the minds of all who met Him.

The Jews were trying to make sense of who Jesus was asserting Himself to be: "We have heard from the Law that the Christ will remain forever, so how can you say, 'The Son of Man must be lifted up'? Who is this 'Son of Man'?"

—John 12:34

Read Mark 8:27–29.

The disciples clearly delivered their answer although it stood against the opinion of the masses. They were prepared to accept Jesus as a prophet but also were willing to go much further and declared Jesus to be the Christ, the long-awaited Messiah.

1. Why do you think Jesus asked for this affirmation from His disciples in Mark 8:27?

Read John 6:14–15.

Throughout Scripture, the title for God's supreme Deliverer, the one who was eagerly awaited by the Jews, was "anointed one" (see Leviticus 4:3; 2 Samuel 1:14). It was frequently used to refer to the king of Israel, as in 1 Samuel 26:11. The Jews were expecting and praying for Messiah, the fulfillment of God's promise that a descendant of David would rule forever (2 Samuel 7:16), one who would deliver them. The primary understanding of this title was "king," a man anointed by God. After the death of King David, Israel hoped for another like him, so their sights were on a man elected and approved of as king and one who was powerful. Kings who came after David continued to disappoint, pushing the messianic age out toward a future hope.

Jesus fused three messianic representations into one—Messiah, suffering servant, and Son of Man. When Jesus refers to Himself as the Son of Man, He is asserting who He is, the promised Savior.

This incident recounted in the passage you just read took place right after Jesus performed the miracle of feeding the five thousand. The Jews saw His power, and many believed he'd be the king they'd anticipated. But He resisted the Jews who wanted to make Him into a commodity, a powerful ruler of the world, a steward of earthly kingdoms. That's not who He was. When we reject who Jesus is, we also are rejecting His revelation, His goodness for our lives. The Jews studied the Messiah and spoke of Him often, yet when He arrived, they clearly missed Him.

A shoot will come up from the stump of Jesse;
>   from his roots a Branch will bear fruit.
The Spirit of the LORD will rest on him—
>   the Spirit of wisdom and of understanding,
>   the Spirit of counsel and of power,
>   the Spirit of knowledge and of the fear of the LORD—
and he will delight in the fear of the LORD.
He will not judge by what he sees with his eyes,
>   or decide by what he hears with his ears;
but with righteousness he will judge the needy,
>   with justice he will give decisions for the poor of the earth.
He will strike the earth with the rod of his mouth;
>   with the breath of his lips he will slay the wicked.
Righteousness will be his belt
>   and faithfulness the sash around his waist.

—Isaiah 11:1–5

EMBRACING THE PROMISE

We have more than one hundred prophecies in the Scriptures that Jesus fulfilled. It is easy to ask how the Jews could possibly miss Jesus being the One. Yet we miss Him all the time because our appetites are not hungry enough for Him. Governing the world was not what God had in mind, but rather governing our hearts. How does the passage from Isaiah 11 put into perspective what we should be asking for?

PRAYER

Lord, I confess to You that my appetites are often counterfeit hunger pangs that will not satisfy me for long. Help me to hold out for Your best and to discern what I need in order to live as a disciple. May I not settle for anything less than what You desire for me. Before I can truly ask for the right nourishment, I have to seek the real You. I thank You that You came to save me and to show me a better way to live. In Jesus' name, amen.

DAY 4

LESS IS MORE

Ask and it will be given to you; seek and you will find; knock and
the door will be opened to you. For everyone who asks receives; he
who seeks finds; and to him who knocks, the door will be opened.

—Matthew 7:7–8

⟫ RECONNECTING WITH THE PROMISE ⟪

Part of becoming a disciple is trusting in God's unconventional ways. He has never
been intimidated by our lack of resources or lack of time to accomplish His plan in
the lives of His people. In fact, it would seem as if He favors working with a deficit. I mean, we see so many underdogs in Scripture conquer. Gideon thought he
needed more soldiers than God did, and God took most of his army away to lead
them to victory. God used Sarah, a barren woman, to produce a people group that
would outnumber the stars. Israel has always been a small country, attacked on every
side by enemies more numerous, committed to their
destruction. Yet today this country still exists, against
all odds.

Isn't it true for us, too, as we look at the deficits
we have to offer God? I personally think marriage is a
relationship through which we become aware of our
weaknesses and a need for *more*. You may have grown
up in a strong circle of faith but married into a family
of mostly nonbelievers. Perhaps you've felt the tension
at times, but in the years of submitting to one another,
God has strengthened your spouse's family through the
heritage you brought through your lineage. God isn't
intimidated by any family tree—remember, Rahab
was in Jesus' lineup! (Read her story in Joshua 2.)
He isn't intimidated by the ill effects of an abusive

Jesus was saying, "Shout to
God. Run to Him. Chase
Him down. Bang on His door
anytime, day or night. Live
higher, with all your heart,
but lean harder on God, with
all that's in you, and you will
find God there—always ready,
ever waiting to give to you—
even beyond what you need."
You can't do it by yourself;
it's impossible, and that's the
whole point. It's not about
us, never has been, never will
be . . . It's all about God.

—Sheila Walsh, *The Shelter of
God's Promises* DVD

father on your life or by any past failures. He loves to make all things new and offer us far more than we could ask or imagine.

Maybe you grew up with only one parent, and sometimes it is hard to think God is fair. Why should you get less than someone else? Resentment toward God grows in you subconsciously. We all can point to where we seem to be lacking. Sometimes we focus on that deficit so much, we cannot see the undeserved blessings that surround our life.

🔲 Examine the areas in your life where you need "more" of something. What resentment might be resulting from your sense of lack in these areas?

⋙ UNDERSTANDING GOD'S PROMISES ⋘

Read Judges 6:11–24.

God uses common people and common things, the least likely to succeed to accomplish His will. Gideon was a farmer, not a soldier, but God called him to deliver Israel from Midian. He was a man full of doubt who lacked faith in God. Yet God used him to change the course of the history of God's people. Gideon had weaknesses and made mistakes: he believed his own limitation would prevent God from working through him; he collected Midianite gold that became an idol; through a concubine, he fathered a son who would bring great

KEY PLACE OF THE PROMISE

Midian—Scholars have not established exactly where Midian is, because the Midianites were nomadic people, constantly moving. The armies of Midian camped in the valley of Jezreel, the agricultural center for the area. They worshipped a multitude of gods.

grief and tragedy to both Gideon's family and the nation of Israel. But his life has many lessons for us: God calls us to obedience, no matter what our circumstances are, and He expands our abilities, despite our limitations and failures.

179

1. In verse 11–13, we see Gideon was going about his daily farming duties. Nothing spectacular was happening. And then the angel appeared. Gideon questions the angel, saying, "If the LORD is with us, why has all this happened to us? Where are all his wonders that our fathers told us about?" (v. 13). He even says the Lord has abandoned them. What can we learn about Gideon from the questions he asks the angel? Are you ever tempted to doubt that God is with you when things go wrong?

> "But Lord," Gideon asked, "how can I save Israel? My clan is the weakest in Manasseh, and I am the least in my family." The LORD answered, "I will be with you, and you will strike down all the Midianites together."
>
> —Judges 6:15–16

2. In verse 14, God says, "Go in the strength you have. . . ." Sometimes we think we have to wait until all circumstances are perfect before we can accomplish anything. In light of your prayer in day 1, what is the strength you have to go and do what He is asking you to do even today? I believe that God calls us as He sees us when we put our trust in Him.

3. In verse 15, we see Gideon's quick reply. What does Gideon point out to God?

4. What is God's promise to Gideon in verse 16?

In chapter 7, Gideon goes on to defeat the Midianites, and God gives him another lesson in trusting in "less" rather than "more." God's "less" is always so much more. Gideon overcomes many of his weaknesses, and he is later recognized in the Hall of Faith in Hebrews 11.

⇒⟫ EMBRACING THE PROMISE ⟪⇐

In scanning over some of God's servants, I'm inclined to think God really prefers operating around our perceived deficits and bringing us to a place of bounty. Here is a list of more people in the Bible just as flawed or afraid as Gideon. Look some of these up and see what God did through weak, common, and discouraged people.

Joseph—a slave saves his family . . . . Genesis 39
Moses—a shepherd in exile leads Israel out of bondage . . . . Exodus 3
Hannah—a barren homemaker becomes the mother of Samuel . . . . . 1 Samuel 1
Mary—a peasant girl becomes the mother of Christ . . . . Luke 1:27–38
Peter—a fisherman who once denied Jesus preaches boldly . . . . Acts 2:14–41

Fill in the blanks in the following statement to reflect you:
_____—a woman who _____ whom God is trying to use to _____.

⇒⟫ PRAYER ⟪⇐

Lord, how freeing to know that less is more in Your eyes. You aren't afraid of my faults, my failures, or limited by my lack. I offer You all that I can to be used for Your glory. Help me to grab hold of this truth and seek You and ask for all I need. In Jesus' name, amen.

DAY 5

LIVING FOR MORE

Ask and it will be given to you; seek and you will find; knock and
the door will be opened to you. For everyone who asks receives; he
who seeks finds; and to him who knocks, the door will be opened.

—Matthew 7:7–8

⋙ RECONNECTING WITH THE PROMISE ⋘

As we continue to set our hearts on the kingdom, there is an "I want more" within us
that remains. We were created for more. The wise author of Ecclesiastes points out
that eternity is set in our hearts (3:11). We know inherently that there is more to life
than what we can see here.

As we seek God, our asking changes. It begins to reflect a different kind of *more*
than perhaps when we first started asking God for things, though often He gra-
ciously gives because He loves us. As we grow toward Him, we sense a connectedness
to our future with God. And we begin to understand there is so much more to our
lives than we can ever imagine. But we know we want more of Him, and we want our
lives to matter for something.

Think about where you are in your life. Are you where you want to be with God,
or do you desire to move toward Him though it involves sacrifice and risk? Maybe
you are finally where you believe God wants you and are experiencing a sweet and
loving intimacy with Jesus.

Jesus is the More who fills the longing for more. We know Him in part, but we
will one day be face-to-face with Him.

▨ If you could ask for more right now and have it, what would it look like?

≫ UNDERSTANDING GOD'S PROMISES ≪

Read Luke 19:1–10.

Zacchaeus was a "chief tax collector," which means he held a higher rank in the Roman tax collection system than Matthew did when Jesus called him to be a disciple. It's clear that he had become a very wealthy man in that region. Jericho was a significant center of commerce, stationed along a major trade route connecting Jerusalem and its surrounding areas with the lands east of the Jordan. We are not told anything about Zacchaeus's personal life, whether he was married or had children, but one thing is clear: he was not a happy man. In Jesus' day tax collectors were the most hated of all citizens, so much so that even beggars wouldn't accept money from them. The idea that Jesus would greet this man and spend any time with him was shocking to the religious establishment.

1. You've heard of "short man syndrome" or a "Napoleon complex." Perhaps Zacchaeus lived some of his life trying to compensate for his short stature by accumulating great wealth. How have you tried to overcompensate for a weakness? What made you discover Jesus was enough?

2. How does Jesus show that Zacchaeus's offering to make wrongs right was acceptable to Him?

≫ EMBRACING THE PROMISE ≪

We began our week looking at Jesus' invitation to us to ask, seek, and knock (Matthew 7:7). But before we close, I want us to look at the verse that comes right after this call:

Which of you, if his son asks for bread, will give him a stone? Or if he asks for a fish, will give him a snake? If you, then, though you are evil, know how to give good gifts to your children, how much more will your Father in heaven give good gifts to those who ask him! (Matthew 7:9–11)

These verses, Matthew 7:7–11, are what is called a *pericope*, which means they stand alone as a complete unit and must be taken together to be fully understood. The illustrations Jesus used here were very significant to the listening crowd.

A small loaf of bread would look just like the small round stones on the lakeshore. The Jews were allowed to eat fish from the sea but not the eels—they were forbidden by their dietary laws. Jesus was saying, Would a father trick his hungry son and give him a stone instead of bread? Would he torment his son by giving him a fish but one he can't eat?

God is not setting you up to trick you or torment you or harm you. God loves you and welcomes you to run to Him with everything that is in you. He is your provider!

⫸ PRAYER ⫷

Father, thank You that You love me more than I will ever understand. Thank You that You long for me to come to You with faith like a child. Help me to look to You for everything I need today, and may Your love spill over to the lives of everyone I touch. In Jesus' name, amen.

> Zacchaeus's life was changed. He gave half of what he had to the poor and if he had cheated anyone, he gave it back to them fourfold. Church history tells us that Zacchaeus went on to become the bishop of Caesarea. He wanted a glimpse of God and became His honored servant. When you pursue God, only He knows what will become of you. Zacchaeus experienced more than he ever thought possible.
>
> —Sheila Walsh, *The Shelter of God's Promises*, chapter 9

THE PROMISE OF HOME

I HAVE A FUTURE

In my Father's house are many rooms; if it were not so, I would have told you. I am going there to prepare a place for you.

—John 14:2

DAY 1

THE PROMISE OF HOME

In my Father's house are many rooms; if it were not so, I would
have told you. I am going there to prepare a place for you.

—John 14:2

As we finish our study together, I want to focus on a promise that extends past this life. Some wounds are hard to heal this side of eternity, so this promise of eternal, forever shelter that God gives us can help us survive any trial in this life. When meeting the basic needs of life has become an overwhelming source of stress, we can rest in the confidence that we'll one day have all our needs provided. When we have lost a brother or sister in Christ whom we love so much that it takes every bit of strength we have just to open our eyes in the morning, we can find joy knowing they're safe in God's home and one day we'll rejoin them there. This promise of shelter is ultimately the promise that we'll live again with Him in glory, and that's a promise we can all look forward to having fulfilled!

VIDEO

25 MINUTES

Watch session 10 on the Shelter of God's Promises *DVD. Keep your Bible nearby for reference and take notes in this book as needed. Fill in the blanks below as you listen to Sheila's message.*

- In my Father's house are many _____; if it were not so, I would have told you. I am going there to _____ a _____ for you. (John 14:2)

- "He has also set _____ in the hearts of men; yet they cannot fathom what God has done from _____ to _____" (Ecclesiastes 3:11).

- For C. S. Lewis, this pull for something more was evidence that something _____, something _____, is what we have all been created for—there is far more than just this life. Something was pulling at him that only the eternal could _____.

He IS the cleft in the rock. Jesus didn't come to _____ us shelter, he came to _____ our shelter.

KEY CONCEPTS

"I tell you the truth, today you will be with me in paradise" (Luke 23:43):

"It is finished" (John 19:30):

MY NOTES

Many moments in life feel unredeemed.

—Sheila Walsh, *The Shelter of God's Promises* DVD

SMALL GROUP DISCUSSION
25 MINUTES

Break into small groups and discuss the following questions:

1. The joys of being a mother are one of the greatest gifts of life this side of heaven. However, life can bring us unexpected sorrows that are difficult to reconcile. Mary experienced the breadth of these worlds. I'm in awe of her strength. Have you ever been in awe of someone's ability to stand strong in the midst of sorrow? Explain a time.

2. Reflect on a few days in your life that you would call the "worst of days." What promises of God meant the most to you during those days?

3. During these ten weeks together, which lesson carried you through some hard days? What did you learn about the significance of that week's promise?

LOOKING DEEPER
10 MINUTES

Dig deeper into Scripture to understand the context of this promise.

This week's promise is a beautiful picture of what life here is leading us toward. This home in heaven, a beautiful house full of rooms for all the brothers and sisters of Christ, is a real thing. It's hard to really grasp that, isn't it? The truth is, though, that we don't know much about heaven because most of us don't study what the Bible tells us about it. We tend to think of heaven in clichés when it's so much more than that.

But the real beauty in this promise, to me, is the fulfillment it gives to those whose lives have felt unredeemed in ways here on earth. When bad things happen to us and they truly can't be fixed, there's hope of a redeemed and perfect life with God in heaven. There is no sadness, no pain, no suffering. Let's study our real home this week so we can get the image of floating on clouds and playing harps with the cherubs out of our heads!

PERSONAL REFLECTION
5 MINUTES

Meditate on the following question and hear what God is teaching you through His Word and through your study group. Share your insights with the group, if you feel comfortable doing so.

> There is no panic in heaven! God has no problems, only plans.
>
> —Corrie ten Boom

What are some things you can't make sense of in this world right now, though you know God's promises are true and He is faithful to carry them out?

LIVING THE PROMISE
5 MINUTES

Discuss ways to apply what you've learned this week with your group.

This will be your last time to meet all together as a group. Take time to share some praises with one another about how God has been faithful to keep His promises, and continue to think about them throughout the week.

PRAYER
5 MINUTES

Take time to pray with your group to close the session.

Focus your prayers around what God has done in your heart to help you receive all ten of these promises. Pray a prayer of blessing over one another as you complete this study.

> When I began to think and pray through this teaching, I had one objective in mind that served as a plumb line as I wrote: *What are the promises of Christ that we can stake our lives on in the best and worst days?*
>
> —Sheila Walsh, *The Shelter of God's Promises* DVD

DAY 2

MY FATHER'S HOUSE

In my Father's house are many rooms; if it were not so, I would have told you. I am going there to prepare a place for you.

—John 14:2

⫸ RECONNECTING WITH THE PROMISE ⫷

Today we will take a look at the promise of our eternal home, our Father's house. I think thoughts about eternity can bring a mix of feelings. Young people want to experience what this life has to offer—a successful career, the blessing of growing a family, and the adventure of traveling the world. But I think the older we get, the more in view and the more relevant this promise becomes: God has a place, your own home in heaven, designed just for you.

What thoughts come to mind when you think about eternity with God? The book of Revelation makes reference to the fact that we will "serve" Him around the throne (Revelation 22:3). So our work is not done in this life. Our lives have purpose beyond this world. Perhaps you have suffered through seasons of thinking, *Life wasn't supposed to look like this*, or *I should have had that opportunity*, or *I should have been able to see my children grow old*. There is more to the story than we have experienced—so much more!

▨ What is hard to comprehend about spending eternity with God?

⫸ UNDERSTANDING GOD'S PROMISES ⫷

Read John 14:1–4.

As Jesus is spending His last evening with the disciples, He offers them relief for the turmoil they are feeling with His approaching arrest. He says in verse 1: "Do not let your hearts be troubled. Trust in God; trust also in me." This is Jesus' final time with them, and He is bringing everything to a head. Their lack of faith and understanding is the cause for the inner conflict they are experiencing. He is telling them to take heart, to trust Him.

> "Now the dwelling of God is with men, and he will live with them. They will be his people, and God himself will be with them and be their God."
>
> —Revelation 21:3

Peter is bewildered, wondering, *Where is He going?* Jesus had spoken to the disciples about going away (John 8:21), but they didn't understand. In the intimacy of this circle of disciples, they are all puzzled. They are frustrated and troubled, and Jesus knows that discouragement and uncertainty have weakened them. He wants to strengthen them against complete collapse, knowing His immanent death is about to be fulfilled.

To move them beyond the dread they are now feeling, He offers them a different perspective. He speaks of a time in the future when they will be reunited. He is showing the purpose for the trouble that is about to descend upon them. If Jesus doesn't leave, then they will never have the benefit of that reunion. So Jesus paints a verbal picture of the Father having a house with many rooms. They will all receive their own rooms. The imagery Jesus uses of a dwelling place (with "rooms") reminds us of the structure of an oriental house where the sons and daughters have apartments under the same roof as their parents. They can trust this to be true because He told them so.

Now, how many of us would accept this logic? Even if it was offered by someone we knew well, we would challenge a statement like this. But Jesus is not like anyone else. The disciples can trust His word as complete and absolute truth, because He has proven this to be the case during three years of close personal contact. Many times Jesus has spoken about the kingdom of God or of a future time without Him, but here He speaks of a future time with Him.

Jesus gives His friends a good reason for His departure: to "prepare a place" (v. 3). It is apparent that eternal life actually has a physical reality to it. The care Jesus has for them extends beyond His time with them on earth. We can count on the reality that there is more to our lives than we experience here on this earth. We can trust all these things to be true, because the very character of Jesus is the proof. We can be certain there is a future for each of us beyond what we are now experiencing.

1. Reading over verse 1, what are some of the tensions you think the disciples were grappling with? What were some of the things that may have been still unsettled in their hearts?

2. There are few verses in the Bible that describe eternal life, but these verses are full of profound promises. What does Jesus tell us He will do?

3. After Jesus gives the disciples this rich promise, Thomas steps forward and asks Him, "Lord, we don't know where you are going, so how can we know the way?" (v. 5). With what Scripture says, what can we know about where we are going with God, even right now?

I think Thomas's words reflect a true disciple. He asks Jesus rather than demands answers. He is honest, showing Jesus he recognizes his ignorance and limited perspective. Without humility we cannot be true disciples. Thomas seems more in tune with a "this world" perspective, which is often how we view our future because it is what we know. Much like we might be thinking, *Okay, God, give me a Google map and Your address. If I don't have Your address, how am I going to find it?* Jesus knew their level of trust in Him had to increase exponentially for them to believe. God is coming back for us and He will show us the way.

⋙ EMBRACING THE PROMISE ⋘

In John 13:37–38, Peter proudly told Jesus that he was ready to die for Him, although later that very night he denied his Lord to protect his own life. It's easy to make promises to God. We know He is faithful to keep His promises to us, but we often experience this truth: "The spirit is willing, but the body is weak" (Mark 14:38). God knows the extent of our commitment to Him.

What promises have you made to God but fallen short of carrying out?

⋙ PRAYER ⋘

Lord, thank You for the promise to live in our Father's house. What a future and a hope we have. My life is secure, and I know that You will show me the best way to Your house from where I am now. Use my life here. I ask for Your blessing over my temporal home here. Please help me to share all I have with others. May my heart be filled with the hope of You and of a future of blessing. In Jesus' name, amen.

DAY 3

JESUS AT YOUR DOOR

In my Father's house are many rooms; if it were not so, I would
have told you. I am going there to prepare a place for you.

—John 14:2

⋙ RECONNECTING WITH THE PROMISE ⋘

In yesterday's lesson, we saw the apprehension and anxiety from the disciples when Jesus spoke this week's promise to them. Jesus knew their hearts were overwhelmed already and He knew they had to be ready for their futures. They had to be ready to receive Him completely.

Further into John 14, Jesus explains, "If you have attained an experiential realization of who I am, you will know My Father also" (see v. 7). By this time, Jesus had presented the Father to His disciples through His life and ministry. They now had a comprehension of the "being" of God.

In verse 8, Philip makes an obtrusive request: "Lord, show us the Father and that will be enough for us." Perhaps Jesus was pleased by his tenacity but saddened by Philip's obtuseness. He responds to His disciple, "Don't you know me, Philip, even after I have been among you such a long time? Anyone who has seen me has seen the Father. How can you say, 'Show us the Father'?" (v. 9). We are like Philip. Part of the purpose of our life here is to prepare us to be with God in the fullest sense. We still find it difficult to recognize Him, to just "be" with Him, to invite Him to "be" in our house and have free rein.

> In light of your experience in seeking God through this study, have you found it easier to just "be" with Him, to not expect a relationship of doing?

⫷ UNDERSTANDING GOD'S PROMISES ⫸

Read Luke 10:3–42.

Luke mentioned that several women who traveled with Jesus and the disciples gave support to the ministry. Jesus' ways transcended the practices of the day, including inviting women to be a part of His ministry. Mary and Martha were women He visited in Bethany (Luke 10:38–39). In essence, the disciples were "homeless" and often needed a safe place to rest and stay. Jesus had no home of His own but found comfort in the homes that welcomed Him. This visit has great potential for the two women to experience personal growth and an opportunity to serve.

In this passage, we see two different women who have taken on two different roles. Martha, the hostess. Mary, the disciple. Jesus is called "Lord" in this passage, which shows they were followers, disciples of Jesus. (You can also see them in John 11:24–27, when Lazarus has died. And Mary is the one who anoints Jesus' body for burial in Mark 14:3–9. They were both active followers of Christ.)

Being with Jesus should have radically diminished the demands Martha felt around the household. Martha also could have felt a bit jealous of her sister. Here she was, trying to fulfill the traditional role of women in those days, and her sister was engrossed in the unconventional role of being a disciple of Jesus, eager to learn from her Teacher.

1. What seems to be the source of Martha's anxiety? In verse 42, Jesus doesn't offer an explanation of "what is better" (v. 42). What do you think He meant?

2. Martha was concerned with preparations and tasks of service. What is her strategy in shaming her sister?

3. The perfect housekeeper may not be the one most inclined to hear God's voice. What distractions keep us from just being with Jesus and being comfortable in His presence?

4. How have you crowded out Jesus from your home? Is He welcome, though you may feel ill prepared to host Him joyfully in your life today?

5. Though Martha sort of gets a bad reputation in this passage, she has strengths we can see. What are the strengths of Martha? Mary?

6. How can we guard against busyness that separates us from Jesus? Has Jesus ever interrupted your schedule?

⟫ EMBRACING THE PROMISE ⟪

Maybe you have been a dinner guest at someone's home and they fussed and went all out to entertain you. But you left hungry for fellowship, because there wasn't time to just be friends and enjoy one another's company. We can strive to do our task list and many things for God, but if we don't take time to be with Him, we cannot truly know the One we are serving and the One we will live with forever. Being with Him transforms us more into His likeness, which purges us from worldly desires, whetting our appetites for heaven.

⟫ PRAYER ⟪

Lord, thank You that You want us to invite You into every room of our hearts. You don't mind the clutter, and we don't have to have everything together before we sit down with You. Thank You for wanting to be with me today. Thank You that Your presence is a promise. Make me more hospitable toward Your Spirit. In Jesus' name, amen.

DAY 4

PITCHING A TENT

In my Father's house are many rooms; if it were not so, I would
have told you. I am going there to prepare a place for you.

—John 14:2

⟫ RECONNECTING WITH THE PROMISE ⟪

If you could build your dream house and had limitless resources, what would it be like? What kind of floor plan would you choose? Would you pick your favorite paint colors or wallpaper to adorn the halls? What would your home say about who you are?

Perhaps you have had the opportunity to build the home of your dreams. However, my guess is there is at least one thing you don't like about your house. It just seems that is the reality of this world. We will always have an experience here of *It isn't quite what I hoped it would be,* or *It isn't quite as fulfilling as I thought it would be.* That is because we were not made to live in our earthly tents for very long. J. C. Ryle reminds us we are traveling to a better place:

> The man who is about to sail for Australia or New Zealand as a settler, is naturally anxious to know something about his future home, its climate, its employments, its inhabitants, its ways, its customs. All these are subjects of deep interest to him. You are leaving the land of your nativity, you are going to spend the rest of your life in a new hemisphere. It would be strange indeed if you did not desire information about your new abode. Now surely, if we hope to dwell forever in that "better country, even a heavenly one," we set out to see all the knowledge we can get about it. Before we go to our eternal home we should try to become acquainted with it.[1]

Somehow we have adopted visions of heaven with cloud-sitting, floating, and lots of harp-playing. Yet Scripture tells us that in heaven we will recognize one another; we will have resurrected bodies. No more cancer, no more divorce, no more heartache! It is the most wonderful promise we have, a promise of eternity based not on our behavior but on the finished work of Christ.

▣ What are some myths or false beliefs you think you've adopted about this place God is preparing for us?

By the end of our study, I think we will all be more than happy to pitch our tent and be in a mode of traveling light because what is ahead is so much better! Throughout this study, we've talked about the importance of allowing the promises of God to be our shelter. We've also identified some ways that the enemy tries to snatch these promises from our hearts. He has done that with this last promise. He has led us to believe many things about this world that are not true, and he has led us to believe many things that are not true about heaven (see Revelation 13:6).

⫸ UNDERSTANDING GOD'S PROMISES ⫷

Read Colossians 3:1 and Hebrews 11:13–16.

Abraham is a big part of the Hall of Faith in Hebrews 11. Abraham knew what it was like to be an alien and a stranger in foreign lands. He pitched many tents in his lifetime. He reminds us we are "aliens and strangers" (see Genesis 23:4). Abraham and the patriarchs only saw the promised land from a distance. Faith is what allowed all the great ones in the Old Testament to see their true citizenship in heaven.

> Most of us find it very difficult to want heaven at all—except in so far as Heaven means meeting again our friends who have died. One reason for this difficulty is that we have not been trained: our whole education tends to fix our minds on this world. Another reason is that when the real want for Heaven is present in us, we do not recognize it.
>
> —C. S. Lewis

1. What is Paul commanding us to do in Colossians 3:1?

2. These people of faith described in Hebrews saw the promise from a distance and welcomed it (v. 13). The reality is we may not have complete resolve here because we are nomads seeking our heavenly reward. How do your unrealized hopes here diminish in light of this passage?

3. In Hebrews 11:14, we see that the people are looking for a country of their own. They don't see themselves as just "earthlings." How can we live our days to reflect the fact that our true home is elsewhere?

Hebrews 11:16 says that God wasn't ashamed of these servants of faith because they understood what they were living for. Heaven has a way of putting this life into perspective. The word *heavenly* connects country with God, to belong to God. He even called Himself the God of Abraham, the God of Isaac, and the God of Jacob. They were family.

4. How did these servants of Hebrews 11 actually do what Colossians 3:1 instructs us to do?

Read 2 Corinthians 5:1–5.

This may be one of the most written-about passages in all the New Testament. Paul is trying to speak of the Christian hope we have, beyond death. We have a future after death. Paul knows he may die before Christ returns again for His people.

We have known Paul as the apostle who spread the gospel with boldness and perseverance, the author of thirteen books of our New Testament. He was also a tentmaker and likened his body to an "earthly tent" that might at any moment be destroyed (v. 1). This didn't discourage Paul, because he was certain of his permanent heavenly home.

5. Paul says we "groan" for our heavenly dwelling (v. 2). This is an intense longing for a better place, a better life. What does your groaning signify? Frustration? Limitation? (See Romans 8:23.)

6. How did Christ's resurrection fuel Paul's hope for a heavenly home?

⇒⟫ EMBRACING THE PROMISE ⟪⇐

Think about the people in your life who are faithful Christians. I think there is a beautiful mystery about people who are serving others and living sacrificially for God. They have their hearts set on eternity. Write down someone you know like this. Review the list of heroes in Hebrews 11, and observe what markers in their lives made it clear what they were living for.

If you could write the final chapters of your life, what would they look like?

⫸ PRAYER ⫷

Lord, thank You for the men and women who have gone before me and set their minds on things above and knew You were the goal of their lives. God, I know You are the one who gives my life meaning and direction, and I thank You for Your promise of eternal life. In Your mighty name, amen.

DAY 5

OUR FUTURE HOME

In my Father's house are many rooms; if it were not so, I would have told you. I am going there to prepare a place for you.

—John 14:2

⫸ RECONNECTING WITH THE PROMISE ⫷

What an amazing way to end a study—with our sights on our future home. We are caught in a tension that has been called "the now and the not yet." Some hard days can seem like we have lived through years of the wandering in the desert. Other days are fleeting, brief moments of joy. It seems we blink and our children are grown. What seemed like a lifetime of waiting on the right man to come along has now resulted in fifty years of marriage. Life can feel much like a dream.

I love the lyrics of a song about heaven by the group Anointed: "Life is a dream, but heaven's reality, and I'm caught in between. I know it seems this world has everything, it's nothing more than a dream."[2]

We often live with this idea in reverse. We think heaven is but a dream, and this life is the full extent of reality.

Have you ever reflected on the promises of God that we will experience in heaven with greater fullness? Review the ten promises we've covered in our study. Comment with a quick phrase or sentence how these promises will be ultimately fulfilled in heaven.

1. The Promise of Jesus

2. The Promise of Provision

3. The Promise of Peace

4. The Promise of Confidence

5. The Promise of Love

6. The Promise of Grace

7. The Promise of Hope

8. The Promise of Strength

9. The Promise of More

10. The Promise of Home

⋙ UNDERSTANDING GOD'S PROMISES ⋘

Sometimes it is hard to fathom what exactly we will do when we make it home to heaven. Scripture does give us some idea about our future home. Even under the curse of the Fall, humanity has created magnificent buildings, amazing art, entrancing music. Can heaven top the creativity we have experienced here? What about shattered dreams? Will God restore the lost opportunities we missed along the way?

Read Ephesians 2:10 and Revelation 7:15.

1. According to these two verses, what will we be doing in heaven?

Read Revelation 22:1–5.

Revelation is a book that many avoid and even fear. But God tells us those who read it and keep its words will be "blessed" (Revelation 22:7). The author is thought to be John, the beloved disciple. The book is full of mystery and intrigue, and clearly it is a book about the end of the age. Revelation unveils and reveals. John was a skilled writer to capture the visions God showed him to communicate the revelation he received. The book ends with a blessing on those who remain faithful to God.

Revelation is often called an "apocalyptic" book, derived from the Greek word *apokalypsis*, meaning "revelation." Though it is a perplexing book, God doesn't want us to avoid reading it.

2. What tree is found in heaven that was in the garden of Eden? (See Revelation 22:2; Genesis 3:22–24.)

3. What are some of the curses of sin? What do these verses tell us about the reverse of sin in heaven?

4. The passage says we will "reign forever and ever" (v. 5). God gave us the mandate to govern the earth and name the animals back in the garden of Eden. How might our influence be exponentially different in heaven?

God does give us many blessings and joys to sustain us in this life. But complete bliss and happiness are not something we usually experience for more than a few days. We can hardly imagine what it would be like to have uninterrupted happiness for a week, let alone for eternity.

Think about the measuring stick you are using to determine if your life is successful. Do you quickly turn to all of life's regrets? I know many believers who are disappointed with their life, in spite of their relationship with God. They don't like how things have turned out. The shattered dreams have left them bent toward bitterness.

But the truth is, no matter what we've done or what we've endured, our goal is to become like Christ. That is the true mark of success. So the pain, the disappointment, the trouble are all part of our life here. And God has given each of us the opportunity to grow toward Him with every situation that comes along. Our path should be one illumined by His light: "The path of the righteous is like the first gleam of dawn, shining ever brighter till the full light of day" (Proverbs 4:18).

5. How has your perspective on life changed in reflecting on the promises studied this week? Have you developed a slight feeling of homesickness, a yearning for eternity with God?

6. Think about a painful hardship you are in or coming out of. How does this put life's disappointments in proper perspective for you? Though you may feel you have failed, can you discern or have a vision of how God might use this experience to change you more to reflect the likeness of Christ?

⫸ EMBRACING THE PROMISE ⫷

I want to leave you with one of the most beautiful passages in all of Scripture, the vision we long to behold with our eyes, where pain will be a distant memory:

> Then I saw a new heaven and a new earth. . . . And I heard a loud voice from the throne saying, "Now the dwelling of God is with men, and he will live with them. They will be his people, and God himself will be with them and be their God. He will wipe every tear from their eyes. There will be no more death or mourning or crying or pain, for the old order of things has passed away." He who was seated on the throne said, "I am making everything new!" Then he said, "Write this down, for these words are trustworthy and true." (Revelation 21:1–5)

How has God made you new through this study?

⋙ PRAYER ⋘

God, what a privilege to pore over these promises. You have been faithful to speak, to teach me, and to strengthen me to find shelter in You and to push me toward the hope of my future. Use me now, and may I spur on those around me to seek You so I can take as many people with me as I possibly can to my future home with You. In the name of Jesus, the real Promise, amen.

NOTES

Introduction

1. Sheila Walsh, *The Shelter of God's Promises* (Nashville: Thomas Nelson, 2010).

2. The Promise of Provision

1. Eugene Peterson, *Working the Angles* (Grand Rapids: Eerdmans, 1987), 30–31.

3. The Promise of Peace

1. Dallas Willard, *The Divine Conspiracy: Rediscovering Our Hidden Life in God* (New York: HarperCollins, 1997), 118.
2. John R. W. Stott, *The Message of the Sermon on the Mount* (Downers Grove, IL: InterVarsity Press, 1985), 50.
3. Oswald Chambers, *My Utmost for His Highest*, "The Key to the Missionary Message," October 15. Public domain.

4. The Promise of Confidence

1. L. B. Cowman, *Streams in the Desert*, rev. ed. (Grand Rapids: Zondervan, 1999), October 24.
2. John Calvin, preface to *Commentary on the Book of Psalms*, trans. James Anderson, vol. 1 (Grand Rapids: Eerdmans, 1948), pp. xl-xli.

5. The Promise of Love

1. Ignatius to the Romans 7:2; cf. Galatians 6:14.

6. The Promise of Grace

1. Dietrich Bonhoeffer, *The Cost of Discipleship* (Austin, TX: Touchstone, 1995), 43.
2. Ibid., p.44.
3. Matthew Henry, *Matthew Henry's Concise Bible Commentary*, originally written in 1706–1721, public domain, exegesis of and commentary on Matthew 22:1–14.

8. The Promise of Strength

1. Amy Carmichael, *Though the Mountains Shake* (Neptune, NJ: Loiseaux Brothers, 1946).

9. The Promise of Hope

1. C. S. Lewis, *The Weight of Glory* (New York: HarperOne, 2001).

10. The Promise of Home

1. Alcorn, Randy, *Heaven* (Carol Stream, IL: Tyndale, 2004), 5.
2. "Life Is a Dream," words and music by Da'dra Crawford Greathouse and David Mullen, released January 1, 1995, Word Entertainment.

ABOUT THE AUTHORS

Sheila Walsh is a communicator, Bible teacher, and best-selling author with more than four million books sold. A featured speaker with Women of Faith, Sheila has reached more than three and a half million women by artistically combining honesty, vulnerability, and humor with God's Word.

Sheila is the author of the best-selling memoir *Honestly* and the Gold Medallion nominee for *The Heartache No One Sees*. Her latest release, *Beautiful Things Happen When a Woman Trusts God*, includes a twelve-week Bible study. She released her first novel, *Angel Song*, and has written several children's books, including *Gigi, God's Little Princess*, which has a companion video series that has won the national Retailers' Choice Award twice and is the most popular Christian brand for young girls in the United States.

Sheila cohosted *The 700 Club* and her own show, *Heart to Heart with Sheila Walsh*. She is currently completing her master's in theology and lives in Dallas, Texas, with her husband, Barry; son, Christian; and two little dogs, Belle and Tink.

Visit her Web site at www.sheilawalsh.com.
Facebook: www.facebook.com/sheilawalshconnects
Twitter: @sheilawalsh / www.twitter.com/sheilawalsh

* * *

Tracey D. Lawrence (M.A., D.Phil.) is an author and founder of Scribe Ink, Inc. She holds a B.S. in Christian education and an M.A. in church history and theology, and she has earned a doctorate in philosophy. Tracey has served as a collaborator for Chuck Colson, Rebecca St. James, Gary Smalley, and others. Visit *www.scribeink.com* for more information about her work.

Tracey lives with her husband, Noel, and son, Jack Brennan, in Greeley, Colorado. Currently, she serves as a board member for the Center for Church Renewal.

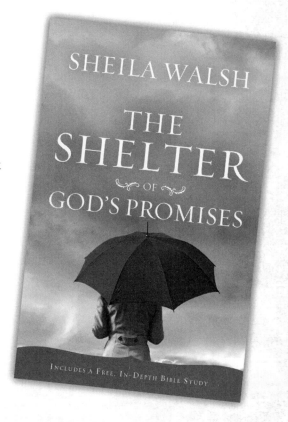